CLAN DONALD'S
GREATEST DEFEAT

ABOUT THE AUTHOR

John Sadler is a retired lawyer. He is married with two daughters and lives in Northumberland. His other books include *Scottish Battles* and *Border Fury: The Three Hundred Years War 1296-1503*. His next book, *Clan Cameron: A History 1164-2005*, will also be published by Tempus.

CLAN DONALD'S
GREATEST DEFEAT

JOHN SADLER

TEMPUS

This book is dedicated to Robert

First published 2005

Tempus Publishing Limited
The Mill, Brimscombe Port,
Stroud, Gloucestershire, GL5 2QG
www.tempus-publishing.com

British Library Cataloguing in Publication Data.
A catalogue record for this book is available from the British Library.

ISBN 0 7524 3330 X

Typesetting and origination by Tempus Publishing Limited
Printed in Great Britain

Contents

Acknowledgements

I must suppose that the most longstanding debt I owe in relation to this book is to my late father and also to my father-in-law, to whom it is dedicated. Though neither may claim to be wholly Scots by birth, both shared a deep and abiding love for the west coast of Scotland, the Highlands and Islands. From my early childhood summer holidays were spent touring in a Sprite Musketeer fourteen-foot four-berth caravan, towed, in stately and unhurried manner, by a succession of sober, grey-hued Austin Cambridges. In those seemingly distant days the intrepid caravanner had some of the aspects of the pioneer and was generally able to establish his caravanserai more or less at will, free of the grim fetters of modern regulation.

The long finger of Kintyre, looking over toward Jura and the relatively inaccessible fastness of Ardnamurchan, was a favoured destination and, to any boy with a romantic disposition, the echoes of the Lordship of the Isles were to develop a particular resonance. On an altogether rarer excursion to the east we came, by way of Inverurie, to the Harlaw battlefield, the squat granite column lowering over the peaceful fields. This seemed so distant a place from the west, the cultures so varied as to be almost alien, and from that my interest in the Reid Harlaw was born.

For their more recent support I must thank Joanna de Vries at Tempus for her unfailing courtesy and enthusiasm; James Chorley who prepared the map and battle plan; the late David Winston for his encouragement and boundless enthusiasm; Cron Mackay for enlightening me on aspects of early-medieval naval warfare; Tobias Capwell of Glasgow Museums; Charlotte Chipchase of The Royal Armouries, Leeds; Helen Nicoll of the National Museum of Scotland; David Edge and Melanie Oelgeschlager of the Wallace Collection; Ailsa Mactaggart of Historic Scotland; Shona Corner of the National Gallery of Scotland; Gwen McGinty of Aberdeen City Archives; and David Bruce of Inverurie Local History Society.

Lastly, and as ever, I would like to thank my wife Ruth for her endless patience and support, without which this book would not have been written. Any errors and inconsistencies remain entirely the responsibility of the author.

Northumberland, August 2004

Timeline

c.503   Kingdom of Dalriada founded.

597   Death of St Columba.

787   Norse raids begin.

858   Kenneth MacAlpin unites Picts and Scots, becomes king.

1058   Accession of Malcolm III of Scotland.

1066   William the Conqueror takes English throne.

1072   Malcolm submits to William.

1098   Magnus Bareleg raids the Western Isles.

1124   Accession of David I.

1138   David defeated at the battle of the Standard near Northallerton.

1164   Defeat and death of Somerled at Renfrew.

1214   Accession of Alexander II.

1249   Accession of Alexander III.

1286   Death of Alexander III.

1292   Accession of John Balliol.

1296   Start of Wars of Independence.

1297   Battle of Stirling Bridge.

1298   Battle of Falkirk.

1304   Siege of Stirling Castle.

1305   Death of William Wallace.

1306   Bruce rebels; murder of John Comyn; Bruce defeated at Methven.

1308   Bruce defeats Macdougalls at the battle of the Pass of Brander.

1314   Battle of Bannockburn.

1328   Treaty of Northampton.

1329   Death of Bruce; accession of David II (as a minor).

1332	The 'Disinherited' battle of Dupplin Moor.
1333	Battle of Halidon Hill.
1338	Beginning of the Hundred Years War.
1341	Return from France of David II.
1346	Battles of Crécy and Neville's Cross; capture of David II.
1354	John of the Isles assumes title of 'Lord of the Isles'.
1356	Battle of Poitiers; capture of John of the Isles.
1357	David II returns from captivity.
1371	Death of David II; accession of Robert II.
1380	Death of John of the Isles; Donald, eldest son by his second wife, assumes the Lordship.
1390	Accession of Robert III; 'Wolf of Badenoch' sacks Elgin.
1402	Seizure and murder of Sir Malcolm Drummond.
1404	Alexander Stewart seizes the earldom of Mar.
1406	Death of Robert III; capture by the English of Prince James (James I); Albany assumes regency.
1411	Battle of Harlaw.
1420	Albany's son Murdoch assumes regency on his father's death; Alexander becomes 3rd Lord of the Isles.
1421	Earl of Buchan defeats English at Beauge.
1424	James I returns from captivity and assumes full control; fall of the Albany Stewarts; Earl of Buchan killed at Verneuil.
1429	Alexander succeeds to the earldom of Ross.
1431	Mar defeated at Inverlochy.
1435	Death of the Earl of Mar.
1437	Murder of James I and accession of James II.
1449	John Macdonald becomes 4th Lord of the Isles.
1452	Murder of the Earl of Douglas by James II.
1455	Battle of St Albans; Wars of the Roses begin in England; James II defeats Douglases at Arkinholm.
1460	Death of James II at the siege of Roxburgh; accession of James III.
1461	Battle of Towton; Edward IV becomes king in England.
1464	Battle of Hexham.
1471	Battles of Barnet and Tewkesbury.
1476	Forfeiture of the earldom of Ross.
1482	Richard of Gloucester takes Berwick; James III's favourites purged at Lauder by Douglas (Archibald, 'Bell the Cat').
1483	Gloucester usurps throne of England as Richard III.

1485   Defeat and death of Richard III at Bosworth; Henry Tudor becomes King Henry VII of England.

1488   Defeat and murder of James III at Sauchieburn and accession of James IV.

1493   Fall of the Lordship of the Isles.

Clan Donald's Call to Battle at Harlaw

(after the Gaelic of Lachlann Mor MacMhuirich, 1411)

You Clan of Conn, remember this:
Strength from the eye of the storm.
Be at them, be animals,
Be alphas, be Argus eyed,
Be belters, be brandishers,
Be bonny, be batterers,
Be cool heads, be caterans,
Be clashers, be conquerors,
Be doers, be dangerous,
Be dashing, be diligent,
Be eager, be excellent,
Be eagles, be elegant,
Be foxy, be ferrety,
Be fervid, be furious,
Be grimmer, be gralloching,
Be grinders, be gallopers,
Be hardmen, be hurriers,
Be hell-bent, be harriers,
Be itching, be irritants,
Be impish, be infinite,
Be lucky, be limitless,
Be lashers, be loftiest,
Be manly, be murderous,
Be martial, be militant,
Be noxious, be noisiest,
Be knightly, be niftiest,

Be on guard, be orderly,
Be off now, be obdurate,
Be prancing, be panic-free,
Be princely, be passionate,
Be rampant, be renderers,
Be regal, be roaring boys,
Be surefire, be Somerleds,
Be surgers, be sunderers,
Be towering, be tactical,
Be tip-top, be targetters,
Be urgent, be up for it,
In vying be vigorous,
In ending all enemies.
Today is for triumphing,
You hardy great hunting-dogs,
You big-boned braw battle boys,
You lightfoot spry lionhearts,
You wall of wild warriors,
You veterans of victories,
You heroes in your hundreds here,
You Clan of Conn, remember this:
Strength from the eye of the storm.

Robert Crawford

I

Being Introductory

From camp to camp through the foul womb of night
The hum of either army stilly sounds,
That the fixed sentinels almost receive
The secret whispers of each other's watch,
Fire answers fire, and through their paly flames
Each battle sees the other's umbered face.

William Shakespeare, *Henry V*, Act 4, Prologue

The Bass of Inverurie at dawn on 24 July 1411: the air around the ancient motte is alive with sounds of war, the gaily striped pavilions of the lords clustering at the base while the tents and bothies of the commons sprawl along the banks of the Don. Odours of sweat, smoke, human and animal waste cloy the cool of a summer's morning. First light and the camp is astir: 'the armourers, accomplishing the knights / With busy hammers closing rivets up, give dreadful note of preparation' (*Henry V*, Act 4, Prologue).

Oatmeal washed down with spirits; sergeants bellowing orders shuffling the unfamiliar companies into order; the dull hues of Lowland spearmen and burghers enlivened by the flash of saffron and plaid; Scots and Gaelic intermingled. Townsmen raising their unfamiliar staves while the wild caterans don their mail and heft their long bladed swords with practised ease.[1]

Finally marshalled into brigades, the army moves off, through the ribbon of the town by beat of drum, over the bridge and along the rutted track of the King's Highway, sweating to gain the plateau past the 'ferm toun' of Balhalgardy. The column of toiling men is now shrouded by a pall of dust; no sign of the enemy. Then, ascending the rim of the higher ground, the plain of broom and furze stretches away, dotted with a patchwork of small fields and enclosures, and there is the Highland host, less than a mile away, the great camp already astir. A steel-tipped avalanche of warriors spills over the plain; men shuffle from column into line in dense, packed schiltroms, spear-points bristling, the caterans deploying around their captains; the banners of the Earl and chivalry of Mar billow proudly.

Steadily the van continues its advance; a man may only see what is happening to his immediate front, with a glance at his comrades left and right, his throat dry, bladder and bowels loose. The enemy swarm speeds closer, a wild, alien race of screaming chants and bearded faces. Adrenalin courses through veins and the red mist of battle descends, the clash of spears like the roaring breakers crashing on the shore.

The 'Reid' Harlaw has long been commemorated as a singularly hard-fought and bloody encounter – a vicious day-long slogging match which, in its fury and duration, far exceeded most battles of the medieval era. The historian John Major, writing in the sixteenth century, commented on the children's game of 'Harlaw' played during his time at Haddington Grammar School in Aberdeen. The 'Heroes of Harlaw' are still an annual toast. The day also, not unsurprisingly, found its place in the annals of Clan Donald, where it was celebrated as a victory for the Gael.

The earliest near-contemporary account is contained in the anony-mous poem 'The Battel of Harylaw'.[2] This is very much a Lowlanders' view in which Mar takes the initiative, attacks the Highlanders and, despite some initial reverses and a long sanguinary fight, takes the field. In so doing, the poet believes the Earl has saved the Lowlands from an orgy of rapine and slaughter.

It is to be regretted that the battle was fought at a time when the great historians of earlier generations, Fordun and Barbour, were both dead; Wyntoun, who might have covered the campaign, chose to conclude his chronicle before 1411. Bower, the Abbot of Inchcolm, writing in the 1440s, does attempt a continuation; he makes no attempt to conceal his partisan view and loathing for the Highlanders: '...by Christ he is not a Scot to whom this work is unpleasing'.[3]

These early Lowland references, based largely on an oral tradition, create the image of a barbarous impi of wild Highlanders bent on spoil and destruction, flinging themselves on the redoubtable spears of honest Lowlanders who have mustered in defence of their homes. Major subsequently attempted to arrive at a more balanced view when he wrote in 1527:

> In the year fourteen hundred and eleven was fought that battle, far famed among the Scots of Harlaw. Donald, Earl of the Isles, with a valiant following of Wild Scots ten thousand strong, aimed at the spoiling of Aberdeen, a town of mark, and other places; and against him Alexander Stewart, Earl of Mar, and Alexander Ogilvy, Sheriff of Angus, gathered their men and at Harlaw met Donald of the Isles. Hot and fierce was the fight; nor was a battle with a foreign foe, and with so large a force, ever waged that was more full of jeopardy than this; so that in our games, when we were at the Grammar School [of Haddington], we were wont to form ourselves into opposite sides, and say that we wanted to play at the battle of Harlaw. Though it be more generally said among the common people that the wild Scots were defeated, I find the very opposite of this in the chroniclers; only, the earl of the Isles was forced to retreat; and he counted amongst his men more of the slain than did the civilised Scots. Yet those men did not put [him] to open rout, though they fiercely strove, and not without success, to put a check upon the audaciousness of the man. They slew his second in command, Maklane [MacLean] and other nine hundred of his men, and yet more were sorely wounded. Of the southerners some six hundred only lost their lives, of whom some were gentlemen, William Abernethy, eldest born and heir to the lord Saltoun, George Ogilvy, heir to the lord of that name, James Skrymgeour, Alexander of Irvin, Robert Malvile, Thomas Muref, knights; James Luval, Alexander Stirling, with other gentlemen of lesser fame. But inasmuch as very few escaped without a wound, and the fight lasted long it is reckoned as hot and fierce.[4]

This lasting vision of the battle as a clash between the civilised Scots, the Lowlanders, and their altogether wilder Gaelic contemporaries has continued to colour subsequent accounts of the battle – a straightforward contest involving racial types. This view is perhaps not entirely without foundation. There was a growing resentment among the magnates of the north-east at the unchecked activities of Highland mercenaries or caterans. However, the principal employers of these freelances were the lords themselves; Mar's father Alexander Stewart, Earl of Buchan, better known by his grim nickname of the 'Wolf of

Badenoch', made much use of caterans as, in his wilder days, had his son: 'a leader of caterans'.

The essentially pejorative view of the Highland clans was, nonetheless, a later manifestation, and anti-Gael sentiment was probably far less of a factor in the fifteenth than in following centuries. It would be grossly simplistic to view the battle in a similar light to, say, Culloden in 1746, when the Lowlanders' contempt for the Gael, the '*mi run mor nan Gael*', had reached its zenith. At Harlaw caterans fought on both sides; Donald of the Isles had never led a campaign before, while Mar had a highly colourful past and his assumption of the earldom was by a *coup de main* rather than any form of legitimate succession.

It is possible to view the battle quite simply as a feudal dispute between leading magnates, exacerbated by the fact the kingdom was without a king – James I was a prisoner in England. The ruthless rapacity of the Albany Stewarts was thereby unchecked and Donald may have been driven to take up arms by the perceived threat of the regent's plan to snatch the earldom of Ross. The battle could also be viewed as an episode in the continuing war between England and Scotland, with Henry IV seizing an opportunity to exploit divisions in the Scottish polity. As a further twist, Donald may have received encouragement from the captive James, who had no cause to love Albany and who would welcome the regent's discomfiture.

It cannot be said that the battle precipitated the collapse of the Lordship of the Isles: this was to endure for another eighty-odd years. Nor did it imply the Lordship was unable to offer military resistance to the Crown. Mar, leading a royal army, was himself worsted at Inverlochy in 1431. Dr Douglas Simpson comments on the distortions heaped upon the events of 1411 by subsequent writers:

Few events have suffered more, in the judgement of posterity, from a false historical perspective. The great battle has often been depicted as a death struggle between two irreconcilable races, as the critical and cardinal contest which forever decided the supremacy of Teuton over Celt in Scotland. Yet Harlaw had its origin in a purely feudal dispute about an earldom – a dispute turned to good account by the English King, so that in its broadest aspect the battle may be properly viewed simply as 'an incident in the uneasy relations of England and Scotland.' It was a mere chance that one of the claimants to the Earldom of Ross should be a Highland chief who sought to enforce his claim at the head of a Highland host.[5]

It is probably fair to surmise that the fear of Highlanders experienced by the solid citizens of Aberdeen in the fifteenth century was a localised concern over the unchecked activities of cateran bands rather than a defined loathing of Gaeldom in general. Undoubtedly the approach of Donald's army produced a reaction, as the approach of an English force would have done. Aberdeen and the east coast had hitherto suffered far more depredations at the hands of the English than at those of the Highland host. Nonetheless, the fact that this was a Highland army imparted to the battle its unique character. Although, as previously mentioned, caterans fought on both sides, Donald's army was different in composition, appearance, outlook and tactics; a clash of cultures did occur, but it took place as a result of a purely feudal rather than a racial dispute.

There must also be doubt as to whether it was Donald's intention to sack Aberdeen. His campaign was not a mindless *chevauchée* aimed at garnering loot and grabbing at any chance for glory. He had taken up arms to enforce what he believed to be his feudal rights, a decision he had not taken lightly. It was true that he had torched Inverness, but this may be viewed as a calculated act of defiance and retribution aimed at the regent's authority.

There is no evidence to support a view that he intended to lay waste Aberdeen and the Garioch; it is more likely he simply intended to assert his authority in those areas which formed part of the earldom of Ross. Donald was not a freebooter in the mould of his more energetic Norse ancestors, but the educated son of a major feudal magnate, one who had achieved his political objectives through guile and diplomacy rather than by the edge of the sword.

A general summary of the facts which may be agreed upon is that in the summer of 1411 Donald, Lord of the Isles, invaded the earldom of Ross to enforce his claim, through right of his wife, to the title. His army, perhaps as many as 10,000-strong, destroyed Inverness and brushed aside all opposition until they entered the Garioch and made camp by the settlement or 'ferm toun' of Harlaw on the evening of 23 July. The following morning the Earl of Mar led a primarily Lowland army up from Inverurie and attacked.

The fight which ensued was long and hard and the issue hung in the balance all day. When the battered and exhausted combatants finally drew apart in the evening, both sides had suffered heavy loss and neither, at that juncture, could claim the field. Under cover of darkness

Donald withdrew, leaving Mar in possession. Aberdeen was thus spared any threat of a Highland onslaught.

These events must be considered in the wider context of, firstly, feudal relationships in early-fifteenth-century Scotland, the rapacity of the Albany Stewarts and the absence of royal authority. Secondly, the battle should be examined as an event in the wider context of the long wars between England and Scotland. The first War of Independence had raged from the Edwardian invasion of 1296 to the successful negotiation of the Treaty of Northampton in 1328.

Following the death of Robert Bruce, the failure of the treaty to deal conclusively with those who had thereby forfeited their cross-border estate, the 'Disinherited', led to a further outbreak of hostilities in 1332. The then Earl of Mar, as regent, and many of the nobility fell in the twin defeats of Dupplin Moor (1332) and Halidon Hill (1333), where King Edward III of England demonstrated the tactical developments that would reap a harvest of notable victories in France after 1338.

Both Robert II and Robert III had been drawn into renewed hostilities when England and France again took up arms after 1369. A new generation of Scottish leaders, the earls of Douglas and March, had wrested the tactical initiative from the English; the 2nd Earl Douglas (also Earl of Mar) won a resounding posthumous victory over the Percies at Otterburn in 1388. In 1402, however, the Douglas of the day had led a national army to total ruin at the battle of Homildon (Humbleton) near Wooler. Henry Percy ('Hotspur') had his revenge for the defeat at Otterburn, though the laurels for tactical skill in both victories probably lie with the Earl of March.[6]

In the same year Robert III's brother, the Earl of Fife, latterly Duke of Albany, had won a power struggle with the king's eldest son, the Duke of Rothesay. The unfortunate duke died in rather undefined circumstances in Albany's custody after his arrest, as did his leading partisan, Sir Malcolm Drummond. When Robert III, a king for whom history has shown scant respect, finally died, Albany became regent; a younger son, now James I, had been captured, in flagrant violation of the truce, by English privateers and sold on to Henry IV. The Kingdom of Scots was therefore without a king, and the steady hand of strong royal authority, essential in the medieval polity to prevent disputes between magnates escalating into civil strife, was lacking. The consequential potential for discord led to the battle of Harlaw.

The feudal system has been likened to a pyramid, with the person of the king at the apex. Lands were parcelled out to the magnates, described as tenants in chief, usually by charter and by way of a perpetual heritable lease. The land never belonged to the magnate in fee simple – that is, absolutely – but was held of the king on terms defined within the original grant or charter. The barons, in turn, sub-let to the gentry (knights), who further underlet to farming tenants. The pyramid was constructed not on the basis of cash rent but on a series of mutually binding obligations determined according to rank.

The magnate owed feudal, that is military, service to the king and the knight owed his sword to the lord. Further down the chain, agricultural labour replaced military service, so the tenant farmer, by his labours and produce, sustained the knight and, above him, the lord. Where actual rents are specified these appear often to be merely nominal, say a pound of pepper or cumin.[7]

Military service was based upon a number of days' (usually forty) attendance in the year, when the baron and, through him, the king could call on the lance and sword of the knight. Knight service was unpaid, although if the period were to be extended then cash payment by way of wages would have to be forthcoming. In the Edwardian wars in Wales, some magnates chose not to receive wages as, by doing so, they might prejudice their expectations in terms of spoils and the grant of conquered territories. The lords were given fixed quotas of harnessed (armoured) knights they must bring in their train; lesser magnates could undertake to substitute two mounted sergeants for a knight (sergeants, being men at arms, would be less expensive to mount and equip than a knight).

Warfare was never a cheap business and the cost of providing one or more war horses, full mail (latterly plate), sword, shield, lance and helm was high, and rose as the period progressed, full plate harness replacing the earlier mail. It was possible to contract out of knight service by paying a fine or premium, described as 'scutage', whereby the knight bought himself out of his feudal obligations for a cash sum.

The king carried on the business of governance through the various officers of the royal household. Military resources were organised and administered by the constable, while the chamberlain was responsible for finance and audit. The chancellor presided over the king's chapel and religious matters – usually a senior clergyman, he was responsible for the drafting and sealing of state papers, including charters, treaties and other weighty matters. The marischall was charged with leading the heavy horse, the feudal elite who made up the backbone of the host, while the steward was to oversee the management of the household. By the thirteenth century, most of these offices had become hereditary.

Beneath these senior officials there was a host of lesser posts, each having defined responsibility: the doorward (there to see there was no undue rowdiness at feasts and other vinous functions), senior clerks of provend and liverance, the pantler, the forester, the royal huntsmen, the sergeants of spence (their function was the important one of ensuring a plentiful supply of bread and wine).[8]

The leading magnates, the earls, were descended from Celtic *mormaers*; Fife was the senior and the earl's hereditary privilege was to place the new king upon his throne. The *mormaers* ('sea officers') could be likened to the pre-conquest earls of England, who enjoyed vice-regal status and were responsible for defence, taxation and the administration of justice in their respective provinces. Post-conquest in England the term became more akin to that of *comte* in France, a leading landowner who held his lands from the Crown and who, in England, might own parcels of manors in a range of locations. Feudalism came later to Scotland, and by process rather than conquest – the Scottish earls therefore tended to have their estates concentrated in the particular locality.

From the reign of David I, the judicial system was concentrated in the hands of three senior officers, the justiciars, each of whom was responsible for a wide tract of territory: north of the Forth and Clyde, the Lothians and the south-east, the south-west and Galloway. The justiciars were supported by a network of Crown-appointed law officers, the sheriffs, twenty-six of them in all. The office was an English import (from the 'Shire Reeve') and, in time, became hereditary. In addition to his responsibility for the administration of justice the sheriff might also act as a local tax officer and castellan of Crown estate.

Perhaps the most purely physical manifestation of feudalism was the castle, be it an imposing royal or baronial hold or the simpler knightly motte. The Normans introduced the castle to England and latterly to Scotland; the Conqueror brought ad hoc wooden castles in pre-formed sections when he crossed the Channel. The earliest examples in both realms were of the timber motte and bailey. This consisted of a raised earth platform surrounded by a defensive palisade which housed the usual domestic offices, with an adjacent bastion constructed on a steep conical mound, linked by a slender causeway into which the garrison could withdraw and, if necessary, mount their final stand.

The castle was far more than a mere garrison outpost: it was a living symbol of the lord's power and his authority, a centre for local adminis- tration and justice, a muster point in time of war and a base for offensive operations. MacBeth may have been the first Scottish king to import Norman knights as mercenaries; his household or mesnie knights seem to have perished with him during his last fight at Lumphanan. The process really began with the Anglophile David I, and colonisation continued for several generations. In 1130 the king ruthlessly suppressed a rising by the fissiparous lords of Moray and parcelled out confiscated lands to the incomers. One of the principal beneficiaries was a Flemish knight named Freskin who already held manors at Uphall in West Lothian. He received a grant of Duffus where, around 1130, he erected a motte: 'the perfect model of a Norman motte and bailey castle'.[9]

Duffus, like many other mottes (perhaps as many as 250 were built in Scotland), was subsequently rebuilt in stone. Huntly Castle in Strathbogie had been founded by the end of the twelfth century and Duncan of Fife, of Celtic rather than Norman extraction, constructed Castle Urquhart, superbly located in the Great Glen overlooking Loch Ness. Here the builders utilised the contours of the bare rock to create the enceinte. Dumbarton, Stirling and Edinburgh were placed on the precipitous stumps of ancient volcanoes.[10]

Stone castles were not new in Scotland; the earlier Norse invaders had also built in stone, although according to the author of the *Orkneyinga Saga* this was largely due to a lack of available timber, which would oth- erwise be the Vikings' preferred medium. A Norse tower on the island of Wyre in Orkney is probably the oldest dateable stone structure anywhere in Scotland; the Vikings, still dominant in Orkney, Shetland, Caithness and the western seaboard, were quick to appreciate the potential of the new style of castle building. Old Wick, possibly constructed by Harald Maddason, was begun *c.*1150.[11]

By the thirteenth century, many of the earlier timber mottes were being consolidated in stone and these were, in turn, influenced by prevailing French styles. John de Vaux, steward to Alexander II's French queen, Marie de Coucy, built his splendid castle at Dirleton copy- ing (perhaps tactfully) the style of Coucy le Chateau on the Aisne, constructed by his mistress's father, Duke Enguerrand III. Bothwell Castle, on the Clyde, is another Scottish fortress heavily influenced by Coucy.[12]

Kildrummy Castle near the Don, 'the noblest of northern castles',[13] was built by the Earl of Mar as a direct response to further disturbances which had erupted in Moray in 1228. As well as being a residence for the lord and focus of local administration, the castle could serve as a base for the control of territory and a point from which a relatively modest number of mailed horsemen could sweep a large swathe of potentially hostile countryside.

The Norman influence in Scotland was grafted onto the existing Celtic framework. There was no ruthless supplanting brought on by conquest, with the exception of troublesome areas such as Moray. The subsequent encroachment proved pervasive, as Lowland Scotland gradually turned its back on its Celtic heritage and, in due course, came to despise the Gael as a savage and unwelcome remnant. Urbanisation was a further factor, which arrived relatively late in Scotland. Prior to the twelfth century there was hardly any settlement which could qualify for urban status.

When the system of royal burghs was introduced, these tended in the main to be in the east, and while there were flourishing ports on the west coast – Renfrew, Glasgow, Rutherglen, Irvine, Ayr and Dumfries – these tended to be less significant. Stirling, Edinburgh, Leith, Musselburgh, Haddington, Roxburgh and Berwick were achieving prominence. Exports to the Low Countries and Baltic states included hides, wool, timber and fish.

Wool was an important staple, and from the mid-twelfth century onward kings of Scotland strove to cement trading links with judicious marriage alliances to Brittany, Holland, England, France, Flanders, Norway and Denmark. Inverness was renowned as a centre for shipbuilding:

> ...in 1247 for example, a ship was built at Inverness for Count Hugh of St. Pol, whose wife was a relative of the Scottish King. This ship, designed to transport crusaders from the Pas de Calais to the Holy Land, was so large and fine that it caught the attention of the English historian Matthew Paris. But the Inverness shipyards could never have built such a vessel if Count Hugh's order had been unique.[14]

As the flower of nationhood in Scotland began to bloom, the Celtic language retreated. During the Wars of Independence, Gaelic remained the language of the commons, even if French was the preferred tongue of the Norman elite and northern English fast gaining ground in the burghs.

As the fourteenth century progressed, the English tongue came to dominate, certainly in the Lowlands and the south-east. While the kings may have had no fixed, preferred capital, there was a tendency for them to reside far more in the eastern half of the country, at Stirling, Edinburgh or Roxburgh. Berwick, prior to the cataclysm of 1296, was the country's major port, far more important than its nearest English rival, Newcastle, some sixty miles south, by the Tyne.

The Celtic tradition in religion was also in eclipse: hitherto, the realm had as its unchallenged patron saint Columba (Columcille) of Iona. Even in the thirteenth century his reliquary, the *Brechennach*, was carried as a talisman into battle.[15] By the end of the century, Columba had been entirely superseded by St Andrew, an east-coast saint, and Ninian, who was anti-Celtic. Malcolm Canmore's English queen, Margaret, had been canonised in 1250.

The advent of feudalism pushed the Celtic systems of law and government into obscurity; primogeniture, the right of the eldest son to inherit, quickly ousted tanistry, the source of many a feud. Professor Barrow has, however, suggested that medieval Scotland perhaps remained closer to its Celtic heritage than might be supposed.

In the more remote and conservative provinces, such as the wild fastnesses of Galloway, the old ways proved tenacious. Here the ancient Norse-Gael laws of *Wergild* ('blood price') survived. Scottish kings and nobles did not disdain the lengthy genealogies of the bards; linking their bloodline to an ancient Celtic past and family was always the first loyalty. In this, the Norman and Celtic ethics converged. Somerled and his descendants in the west built up their lands and affinities with the same single-minded and ruthless obsession as the Stewarts.

Feudalism is often viewed as a system founded on oppression, with the landed classes living off the labours of a servile peasantry tied to the land. This may be true, and yet in practice the system probably worked more as a partnership. The tenant farmer toiled to work the land, but the knight provided protection and the lord access to justice. The land had to be worked; without efficient agricultural production the system failed. In a sense feudalism was also the reverse of the pyramid, with the producers, at the base, being the key constituent. Besides, not all forms of tenure fitted neatly into the feudal mould. An obvious exception is the proprietary estate called the 'ferm toun'; this was an agricultural holding in the ownership of a number of heritors whose property rights passed by will or survivorship to their children.

The fourteenth century, despite the adverse impacts of the Wars of Independence, witnessed a growth in the size and prosperity of the towns. Trade was on the increase and there was a steady influx of skilled tradesmen from the continent. The majority of the population continued to live in smaller, rural communities, the commons dwelling in cruck-framed timber houses with wattle and daub panels supported on several courses of masonry and roofed with a covering of heather or thatch. The knight might live in a hall, house or tower; the hamlets were linked by a network of miry tracks. Sanitation was basic and lawlessness rife. Visitors generally found Scotland a poor country, although evidence from the late fourteenth century suggests a spell of good harvests; a bad harvest could spell starvation.

Oats and wheat were staple crops, as was barley, which may have accounted for as much as thirty per cent of production. Most of this went into the production of ale or 'small' beer, the water generally being unfit to drink. Cattle were also grazed and the ratio of beasts increased the more marginal the land. After the scourge of the plague mid-century, much marginal land went untilled.

The Black Death altered the socio-economic structure in that it put a premium on labour, so that a farm worker might now command cash wages for his services. Consequently, the number of unfree serfs diminished. By the late fourteenth century, traditional feudalism was under threat from a number of directions. Edward III of England had relied not upon the unwieldy feudal hosts of his grandfather's day but on pared-down armies composed of professional companies, who fought for money under a system of contract or indenture.

As the lords began to rely more upon armed or liveried retainers, the pernicious system of livery and maintenance developed, whereby the followers were no longer bound to the lord by a raft of social obligations but were mere hirelings. This system, known as 'bastard' feudalism, was commonplace by the dawn of the fifteenth century and, in England, would subsequently be viewed as one of the causes of the Wars of the Roses.

In Scotland, the effects of bastard feudalism can be clearly discerned in the north-east in the late fourteenth century, when magnates such as the Wolf of Badenoch and his sons relied, for military muscle, on mercenary caterans, drawn mainly from the Highland clans of the west. This practice, necessary from the lord's point of view to maintain the defence of his lands, would breed resentment from those who suffered from the casual lawlessness of the cateran, and would contribute in no small measure to the Lowlander's increasing resentment toward the Gael.

2

The House of Stewart

Jean Froissart's picture of the decrepit sixty-nine-year-old Robert II in 1384, bowed down with age, bleary eyed, wishing for peace with England but openly despised and ignored by his bellicose nobility, was the earliest and one of the most important elements in the developing of an enduring tradition which saw the first two Stewart kings as weak, ineffective and inadequate monarchs.[1]

Robert II had to wait a long time for his day to arrive; he was the son of Robert Bruce's eldest daughter Marjorie and Walter the Steward, considerably older than his cousin David II. He was very much perceived as 'yesterday's man' when the king died unexpectedly in 1371. He had a long record in public office, although his tenure was by no means distinguished. He had acted as regent while the king languished in captivity following his capture at the debacle of Neville's Cross in 1346. Following David's return, relations between the two had not always been cordial and the Steward's hand was discerned in the dramatic killing of the king's current mistress Katherine Mortimer, stabbed to the heart in the saddle, a murder worthy of Webster or Ford. Medieval Scottish politics tended toward the robust.

The Stewarts were to claim their descent from Banquo, a claim put forward by Hector Boece in his *Historia*. He may possibly have read a lost work by Barbour entitled *The Stewarts Original*, wherein the author, by a prodigious leap of speculation, traces the family tree as far back as Ninus, the legendary founder of Nineveh![2] In more historical terms, the family origin can be traced to Dol de Brétagne in Brittany, where they held hereditary office as stewards to the Counts of Dol. During the tenure of Count Rhiwallon, the steward Alan produced three sons, Alan, Flaad and Rhiwallon.

The eldest followed in his father's footsteps, Rhiwallon took the ton-sure, and Flaad, in the wake of the Norman Conquest, sought his fortune in England and settled on the Welsh Marches. The early twelfth century witnessed an influx of Breton knights who enjoyed the patronage of Henry I; Flaad also owed his advancement to the king and was granted lands by Monmouth. He, in turn, also produced three lads, one of whom, William, became the ancestor of the Fitzalan Earls of Arundel.

The youngest son, Walter, was one of those Norman knights who came to the attention of the future David I while he was at the English court. Returning with him to Scotland, he earned favour and advance-ment, attaining the office of High Steward, a senior position within the king's household. David I later supported Henry I's daughter Matilda in the long civil wars between her and Stephen of Blois; the marcher lords, including the Fitzalans, also championed the Dowager Empress. Walter probably settled in Scotland between 1134 and 1140 and received the barony of Renfrew.

He probably commanded local forces against an invasion from the Highlands led by Somerled, the ancestor of Donald of the Isles. The Steward's mounted knights, despising their Norse-Gael opponents, launched a series of co-ordinated charges which utterly broke the attack-ers; Somerled and one of his sons fell in the ensuing rout.

Walter, now established as a leading magnate, died in 1177 and was succeeded in his office by both son and grandson. The fourth genera-tion of the family to hold high office commanded the royal forces at the battle of Largs in 1263; the battle was in fact a series of relatively minor skirmishes, but the political consequences were considerable. The fifth Steward proved unshakeable in his loyalty to Bruce and wed Cecilia, the daughter of Patrick Dunbar, Earl of March, a highly advan-tageous match. Their son, another Walter, also served his king valiantly and was knighted on the field of Bannockburn where, jointly with Douglas, he commanded one of the divisions of the army on the sec-ond and decisive day of the battle. Barbour wrote glowingly of his conduct on the field:

The lad is young, but none the less
Shall bear himself with such prowess
And show such manliness in war
That tutelage, he'll need no more.[3]

It was this Walter, the sixth High Steward, who married the king's daughter and whose son would ascend the Scottish throne as Robert II. After Bannockburn he won further laurels by his spirited defence of Berwick in 1319, though both he and his wife Marjorie died young – he aged only thirty-four in 1326 and she as a result of a fall from her horse while heavily pregnant. John of Fordun, writing of Robert in his youth, paints a very different portrait from Froissart describing the aged king: 'tall and robust, modest, liberal, gay and courteous; and for the innate sweetness of his disposition generally beloved by true-hearted Scotsmen'.[4]

Initially, before the birth of his heir David, Robert Bruce had nominated his surviving brother Edward as his successor. Edward Bruce, a volatile and ambitious character, led the Scottish intervention in Ireland from 1315 to his defeat and death at the battle of Faughart in 1318. This expedition could be viewed as the opening of a second front against the English in Ireland under the banner of some form of wider Celtic brotherhood. More simply and cynically, the expedition could be seen as a useful means whereby the king removed a potentially quarrelsome sibling from the realm, his death in battle an altogether tidy solution.

The young Robert was blooded in the disaster at Halidon Hill and went on to command the left-hand division of the king's army at Neville's Cross. His conduct during the battle has been questioned since. His brigade withdrew undefeated, even though they had been severely checked by Edward Balliol's mounted charges, and thus left the king's central division hopelessly exposed. The Steward's conduct might have been due to excessive prudence, straightforward faintheartedness or treasonable opportunism. David II inclined to favour the latter, although defeat always breeds a need for scapegoats.

As regent, Robert was not unduly proactive in working toward the king's release, and relations between the two thereafter remained strained. When David's first wife died in 1362, he proposed to wed his mistress, Margaret Logie. The Steward lent his name to a rather half-hearted baronial rising, which was effortlessly suppressed, and the marriage was celebrated in April 1363. Robert and his sons were obliged to submit and crave readmittance into the king's grace. David II died both unexpectedly and without issue on 22 February 1371; Robert the Steward, at the relatively advanced age of fifty-five, became king.

Despite his long captivity in England (1346–1357), or perhaps because of it, David II never displayed any particular Anglophobia; he was by no means enthusiastic about resuming hostilities in 1369. Robert, however, faced a generation of young and aggressive lords who had avoided the disaster at Neville's Cross and who were anxious to exploit the renewed conflict between England and France. Their immediate objectives were to eliminate the English enclaves in the western marches, Teviotdale and the Merse, and to recover such key fortresses as Lochmaben and Roxburgh.

The later picture which Froissart paints of an ageing and hapless monarch ignored by these young warlords may be inaccurate. While Robert II continually talked of peace and gave repeated assurances to England of his pacific intent, he may well have been playing an altogether more subtle game, with Douglas and March the blunter instruments of his policy. If so, he was successful: from 1371 the Scots regained the initiative on the borders and gradually set about pinching out the English salients. This steady attrition has echoes of Robert I's policy prior to Bannockburn, gradually wresting key bastions back from the invader but avoiding set-piece encounters or extensive forays that would provoke massive retaliation.

Robert appears to have divined that the administration of Richard II, beset by reverses in France and with an empty treasury, was not minded to embark on further adventures in Scotland. Active French intervention did spur the English king to invade in 1385 and the Scots relied on their traditional Fabian tactics. Richard had the satisfaction of torching Edinburgh, but his costly campaign produced no lasting gains.

The Scottish campaign of 1388 involved a two-pronged thrust: Douglas and March leading a decoy column through Northumberland while the main blow fell in the west. The ruse was brilliantly successful and ended with an engagement at Otterburn on St Oswin's Eve (19 August). The English, under the impetuous Hotspur, were routed after a hard-fought night battle in which Douglas, leading the decisive flanking attack, was cut down, dying gloriously in the hour of his greatest triumph.

It was during the years of David II's captivity that both England and, latterly, Scotland had been stricken by bubonic plague – 'the Black Death', a lethal and virulent pestilence that first struck in 1349 and was to reappear periodically for the remainder of the medieval era. At first seemingly immune from 'the foul death of England', it is said that a raiding party, with tidy irony, carried the contagion back into Scotland. One of the prime effects of the plague was that labour replaced land as a scarce

resource; with so many gone, an able-bodied agricultural worker suddenly discovered a ready market for his skills. The loss of so much labour
inevitably caused rents to tumble and many previously viable holdings
become economically unsound; this in turn promoted the growth of
larger lordships to effect economies of scale. Bower describes an era of
plenty during the later fourteenth century: 'an abundance of provisions
in the Kingdom'.[5]

Overseas trade also recovered in the reign of Robert II; the customs
dues from wool exports, on which royal revenue was highly dependent,
recovered substantially and reached the levels experienced in the haly-
con days of the 1320s. By the turn of the fifteenth century, however, the
situation was reversed, with income dropping to a mere forty per cent
of that achieved in the 1370s and 1380s; this decline was matched by a
marked fall in the value of the Scots pound.

If Robert II pursued a carefully calculated and successful policy in
relation to the war with England, both he and his son John, Earl of
Carrick (later Robert III)[6] acted, in terms of advancing the Stewart
interest, like other ambitious magnates. The Wars of Independence had
engendered many torn loyalties among the Scots nobility, yet by the
1370s nearly twenty-five per cent of the male lines had, through natural
causes, failed.[7] Both Robert II and Robert III made full use of opportunities through grant, forfeiture and, above all, advantageous marriages.

Robert II had no less than twenty-one children. By the end of his
two decades on the throne, his sons held a clutch of earldoms and all of
his seven legitimate daughters had married into leading magnate families. One daughter was wed to John of the Isles, so that Donald became
a nephew of Robert III. By 1377, seven out of sixteen earldoms were in
Stewart hands; by the 1390s this had grown to twelve.[8] The Stewarts thus
became truly *primus inter pares*, the most powerful and influential affinity
in the realm.

These early Stewart kings were peripatetic, having no fixed capital.[9]
They rubbed shoulders with the nobility and pursued an easy style of
kingship, sometimes referred to as *laissez faire*, with the nobility having
access and the freedom to comment. This was not a sign of weakness.
The Crown avoided any serious revolts until Donald of the Isles raised
his banner in 1411; the war with England quietly yielded dividends; all
of the English salients were gradually eliminated and Roxburgh finally
recovered in 1409.

The constant military activity on the border, albeit much of it low-key or, as it would now be termed, 'low intensity', required the exertions of strongly placed marcher lords: the Douglas in the west, Ker, Hume and March in the middle march, Teviotdale and the Merse. The growing power of the Black Douglas was to lead to conflict in the reign of James II but, in the late fourteenth century, strong baronial families were needed to maintain the initiative wrested from the English. This would continue to be the case with the Scots until the disaster at Homildon in 1402.

In 1381 the ageing king brought his eldest son, John, Earl of Carrick, into his administration; the presence of the heir presumptive was a necessary move to ensure smooth continuity and a seamless transfer of authority on the old king's death. Robert II was now in his mid-sixties, a respectable age for the time, when relatively few men saw out their fifties. The king had, in fact, been married twice. His first wife was Elizabeth Mure of Rowahan, by whom he had four sons. Several of these were still living when the marriage was validated by a papal dispensation on 22 November 1349. Prior to that, the question of consanginuity tainted the legitimacy of the union and thereby the issue. Even after the dispensation was granted, a doubt lingered as to its efficacy and therefore the taint of bastardy hung over Carrick.

The king's second wife, whom he married in 1355, was Euphemia, the daughter of Hugh, Earl of Ross, and the issue of that union, including the surviving son Walter, Earl of Athol, were not subject to the same uncertainty. This could obviously provide Walter and his brother David, Earl of Strathearn with a claim to the succession.[10] The king clearly felt that the matter required a formal resolution and therefore introduced an Act of Succession in 1355, which provided that the Crown would pass firstly to Carrick, then to his male heirs, or failing these to Fife, his male heirs and thereafter to Buchan and his line. Only if all these failed would the throne revert to the king's sons by his second marriage.[11]

Carrick was then elevated to the office of Lieutenant of the Kingdom and within three years appeared to have taken over the reins of power completely, with his father being effectively removed in a bloodless coup. Perhaps the king was becoming senile; there appear to have been concerns within the Scottish polity at the favour being extended to his volatile third son, Alexander, Earl of Buchan. The Wolf of Badenoch was heavily censured by the General Council in 1385; this appears to have arisen from his ready employment of caterans. The chronicler John of Fordun, writing at this time, provides the first pejorative view of the Gael as a 'savage and untamed race, rude and independent, given to rapine... and exceedingly cruel'.[12]

Carrick may have replaced his ageing father but, in 1388, he was himself at least partially disabled as a consequence of a kick from the horse of James Douglas of Dalkeith. Exactly what permanent impairment resulted is unknown, but the handicap must have been sufficient for the exercise of royal authority to devolve onto the capable shoulders of his younger brother, the Earl of Fife (later Duke of Albany). Even prior to his injury, there was some question over Carrick's fitness to govern; he apparently had a depressive and neurotic personality[13] and the accident may simply have served as an excuse to divest himself of responsibility.

Fife's power was by no means absolute. His appointment was, in every sense, constitutional, he being obliged to account on an annual basis to Parliament or the General Council. The arrangement proved highly effective, for when Robert II finally died on 19 April 1390 there was no recourse to anarchy or any serious threat to Carrick's taking the throne as Robert III. The only disturbances came from the north, where the Wolf bared his fangs and unleashed his caterans to sack the Burgh of Forres – even the sacred precincts of Elgin Cathedral did not escape the flames. Such delinquency did not, however, suffice to dent the stability of the realm as a whole.

Robert III married Annabella, the daughter of Sir John Drummond of Stobhall, herself the niece of David II's queen, Margaret Drummond. The queen, while she lived, continued to exercise a restraining influence over her eldest son David, Earl of Carrick and later Duke of Rothesay. A wild and intemperate young man, he had an unenviable knack of making enemies, most dangerously, his powerful uncle Fife, who was to be elevated to Duke of Albany. The queen also bore several daughters, two of whom married into the powerful Douglas clan: Margaret, the eldest, was betrothed to Archibald, later the fourth earl, and a younger girl, Elizabeth, wed Sir James Douglas of Dalkeith.

Bower recounts a story from the coronation and subsequent homage of the magnates which serves to illustrate King Robert's sympathetic nature:

Since the concourse of barons and their retainers was so great as to trample down the ripening crops of the monks, their granger, Robert Logy, endeavoured to complain to the King in person, only to be repelled in derision by the courtiers. Early next day when the court was about to leave Scone, Logy, collecting a band of hinds, returned to serenade the King. Asked for an explanation, he replied this was a demonstration of gratitude for being saved the labour and expense of reaping the year's harvest. The courtiers angrily demanded his punishment, but the King gave orders the damage should be assessed and due compensation paid to the monastery.[14]

Robert, Earl of Fife was the leading politician of his age, perceived as the architect of the successful 'cold' war with England and the recovery of the Pale. He was experienced, calculating, rapacious and utterly ruthless. To all intents and purposes, and with the brief exception of the Rothesay ascendancy, he continued to rule Scotland until he finally died in 1420, by then in his eighties! By 1372 he enjoyed the earldoms of Fife and Menteith and the focus of his personal ambition lay in extending the bounds of the latter. By the middle of the decade he had snapped up the barony of Glen Dochart and Strath Garney on the western flank of Menteith and begun construction of his impressive, near-palatial castle at Doune.

The acquisition of these new lands embroiled him in an acrimonious dispute with Sir John Logie, a son of David II's queen, Margaret Drummond. In 1373 he executed a signal coup by acquiring, in alienation of the rights of the Crown, the constableship of mighty Stirling. Such alienation was a not uncommon feature of the reign of Robert II, when various Crown appointments and resources were granted to local magnates to consolidate their affinity. With Crown revenues from customs dues running at high levels, King Robert could afford to buy friends.[15]

While extending his grip in the west, Fife did not neglect the Highlands. His meddling was to promote significant changes in lordships in the Lennox/Argyll region which would affect the hitherto Celtic establishment in the area. In 1392, after careful cultivation, he arranged for his heir, Murdoch, to marry Isabella, the daughter of Duncan, Earl of Lennox, who was otherwise without a male successor. Isabella was thus the heiress presumptive, and Fife was careful to make certain of his son's prospects by persuading the earl to agree that neither of her two younger sisters would wed without Fife's express consent – effectively ensuring he could veto any likely challengers. On 8 November 1392, a compliant Robert III agreed to the earldom being entailed to Murdoch and his heirs. This was a significant gain, to Fife's base of Menteith was now added the presumption of the adjoining earldom.

Fife now married his daughter Marjory to Duncan Campbell, eldest son and heir to Sir Colin Campbell, lord of Loch Awe and hereditary lieutenant of Argyll between Loch Gilp and Loch Melfort. This constituted another sound investment in the marriage market; the Campbells were a name set to rise, and having the Earl of Fife as a father-in-law could only be advantageous. By the mid-1390s the Campbell chiefs, now styling themselves Lords of Argyll, had achieved a regional prominence, successors to the MacDougall hegemony of the late thirteenth century. In so doing, they were almost in a position to challenge John of the Isles for dominance of the western Highlands.

The emergence of the Campbell lordship and the expansion of Fife's power in Menteith and now Lennox cannot have failed to alarm his equally astute brother-in-law, John of the Isles. Nor was the earl yet done; having secured the Campbell alliance he cast his eyes over Lorn, where John Stewart had aspirations. This Stewart was an ally of Duncan Campbell and was in his train in July 1395 when the earl mounted a progress through his lands in Fife. John's son Robert then married Johanna, another daughter of the earl.[16] Robert Stewart was heir to the lordship of Lorn in northern Argyll, extending to the southern shores of Loch Linnhe.

By these careful alliances, Fife had created an affinity that controlled the west coast from the Firth of Clyde to Loch Linnhe and greatly extended the established holdings of the Stewartry. Murdoch was justiciar north of the Forth and keeper of Stirling; the family appeared to enjoy an inexpugnable position. Even the earl's advancement to his dukedom in 1398 was carefully chosen; Albany was an ancient appellation for all of Scotland north of the Forth. It was an elevation others would deeply resent.

One of these was Fife's younger brother, Alexander Stewart, the Wolf of Badenoch. He had gained lands in the north-east from his father, whilst his claim to Badenoch derived from the terce rights of his second wife Euphemia, widow of John Randolph, Earl of Moray, who had fallen at Neville's Cross. By 1370, Alexander was exercising control, and the grant of the lordship was ratified on his father's accession. Even at this relatively early stage in his career, Alexander's swashbuckling style and employment of caterans was causing disquiet.

Having acquired Badenoch, he now aspired to the earldom of Moray, but the king had determined to subdivide the dead earl's many acres and appointed Alexander's younger half-brother David as Earl of Strathearn. The Wolf was amply compensated for any disappointment when he was raised to the lieutenancy of the north-east, administering all the lands from the northern rim of Moray to the Pentland Firth, including the sheriffdom of Inverness, and excluding only the regality of Moray. Before the end of 1377 David was also created Earl Palatine of Caithness. Robert II was thus careful to advance both of his sons, while simultaneously creating a check on both.[17]

Alexander was the equal of his brother Robert in ambition, although his rough and ready methods lacked Fife's more subtle touch. Further opportunities for Alexander in the north-east arose when William, Earl of Ross died in February 1372. The late earl's daughter and heiress was married to Sir Walter Leslie, who naturally had aspirations to his father-in-law's title, nothwithstanding that the two men had quarrelled and the king was no particular friend of the Leslie faction. Robert II took a portion of the estate under the Crown's direct control and instructed Alexander to maintain the terce rights of the earl's widow, Mary of the Isles. He thus had a significant foothold in Ross, much to the disgust of the Leslies.

In the same year, the Wolf added to his domain by entering into a lease of Castle Urquhart from his brother David as landlord; this gave him a strategic base in the Great Glen. At the same time he was collecting further royal appointments, extending his offices into northern Perthshire, which gave him effective control over a great swathe of the north-east extending to the cold waters of the Pentland Firth. Despite these significant gains, Alexander lacked the impressive array of titles now bestowed on his two older brothers of the whole blood and his younger half-brother.

In the following decade the Lindsay/Leslie affinity was lessened by the death of Alexander Lindsay of Glen Esk, a member of the King's Council and justiciar north of the Forth. He died at Candia on Crete, en route to the Holy Land, and he was swiftly followed by Walter Leslie himself, a noted crusader, who breathed his last at Perth on 30 February 1382.

Alexander was quick to woo his dead rival's widow, Euphemia, and they were wed before the end of the year.

Robert II apparently had no qualms about the transfer of the Countess's lands to his younger son. Others, including Fife, did have reservations, and these were voiced at a meeting of the Council in June 1382. By July, however, the king had progressed to Inverness to officiate at Alexander's installation as Earl of Buchan. Euphemia resigned the lands of the new earldom to the king. These were the holdings associated with the barony of King Edward; the old province of Buchan, a Comyn stronghold, had been broken up by Robert I after he'd dealt with the Comyn faction through the ruthless 'herschip [wasting] of Buchan'.

At a stroke the Wolf had acquired, jointly with Euphemia, the lordships of Skye and Lewis, the thanages of Dingwall, Glendowachy and Deskford, together with an interest in all of his wife's extensive holdings in Caithness, Sutherland, Atholl, Galloway and elsewhere. The terms of the marriage settlement were that the whole of this vast estate would pass to any heirs produced by the union, failing which Euphemia's existing offspring would take them. The earldom of Ross was granted to Alexander in life-rent only; the title would not, therefore, vest in any joint heirs. In fact, as Euphemia was considerably older, there appeared little prospect that she would bear further children. This would be little consolation to her son, Alexander Leslie, who was effectively excluded from his estate for the whole of his stepfather's lifetime – the Wolf himself still being a relatively young man. The Lindsay/Leslie faction had very little to celebrate!

Worse was to follow. The late Alexander Lindsay had held the office of justiciar north of the Forth; the appointment had been shared with his nephew Sir James Lindsay of Crawford and the family might have hoped that either he or the dead man's son and heir Sir David might have succeeded. However, after an interregnum of several years and certainly prior to February 1387, the job went to Buchan.

Lindsay of Crawford proved to be a bad loser and a worse enemy. Possibly in retaliation for this disappointment or, equally possibly, as a result of an unrelated dispute, he murdered Sir John Lyon, thane of Glamis and one of the king's sons-in-law. That he was able to commit this crime with apparent impunity was due to his powerful position in the affinity of the Earl of Carrick. He was also linked to the formidable Douglases, who acquired a stake in the north-east in 1377 when, on the death of his

brother-in-law, the first Earl of Douglas also became Earl of Mar. Douglas
easily persuaded the earl's widow to surrender her terce rights in the
earldom and the keeping of Kildrummy Castle for a relatively modest
annuity of 200 marks and a right to occupy Tantallon Castle, perched
impressively on the sea cliffs of Lothian.[18] Lindsay also had a claim to the
earldom of Buchan which eventually came before the courts.

Buchan now controlled a vast domain and one that extended his sway
into his older brother's heartlands of Lennox and Menteith, into Fife,
Angus and Mar, and took in a haul of sheriffdoms north of the Forth
from Dumbarton to Nairn. The difficulty he faced was that to enforce
order he was obliged to rely on the hire of Highland auxiliaries, the
much dreaded caterans. These troops were not, as they are frequently
described, outlaws; they were mercenary companies employed by northern magnates who did not have Lowland estates from which they could
summon a feudal levy. Quite simply, for a lord like Alexander Stewart
they were the only sure military resource available. This did not render
them popular. The minor gentry of the provinces and the burghers of
Inverness and Aberdeen viewed these uncouth Highlanders with fear
and disdain, to the extent that, in the mind of the Lowlander, the term
cateran was to be synonymous with 'malefactor or evil doer'.[19]

These caterans were drawn from the following or kindred of the great
Highland lords, men such as John of the Isles; their dress, weaponry and
language were both distinctive and alien to the Lowlanders. They may be
likened to their contemporaries in Ireland, the 'kernes', who appear in
the service of the Anglo-Irish magnates. Buchan, having engaged these
native mercenaries, had to pay them and provide sustenance; this led to a
requirement for free quarter among his tenantry. The billeting of troops
on a civilian populace has never been popular; standards of discipline
were undoubtedly questionable and outrages may have occurred.

The unchecked depredations of some of these cateran bands appears to
lie at the root of the disputes between the earl and the bishops of Moray
and Aberdeen, who were vociferous in their loud indignation, motivated
by the need to protect Church lands. This indignation is echoed in the
later writings of the sixteenth-century chronicler Hector Boece, who
claims the Wolf was a cateran: 'whose wickedness had earned him universal hatred'. He was 'joined by certain vile creatures and… drove off all
the bishop's cattle and carried away his property, killing at the same time
in the most high handed way the peasants… He divided as he pleased

the lands stolen from the church, and gave them to be cultivated by certain wicked men who had no regard for God or man.'[20]

Despite the swelling chorus of protest, the king continued to support his son in office. In so doing he damaged his own standing, for a clear perception was emerging that Buchan, the justiciar, was a large part of the problem, rather than representing any form of solution. The Wolf, in the opinion of his neighbours and tenants, had gone native, identifying himself with the Gael rather than the Teuton. He was, to his cateran followers, *Alasdair Mor Mac An Righ* ('Great Alexander the king's son'). The fact was, however, that virtually none of the northern earldoms were held by men with any Gaelic connection. Many were also absentee landlords, so Buchan's only avenue for building up his own affinity involved cultivating the Gael. This would equip him admirably with military muscle but would earn the opprobrium of Lowland society, headed by the powerful voice of the Church.

When Carrick was appointed Guardian, the earl's critics, headed by the vengeful Lindsay, were ready to strike. The Great Council of 1385 heavily censured the Wolf for his abuses of Crown office, his intemperate employment of caterans and the questionable nature of certain of his land acquisitions. Lindsay instigated proceedings for the recovery of Buchan, and David of Strathearn strove to recover possession of Castle Urquhart.

Despite, however, the seriousness of these assaults, Buchan emerged remarkably unscathed and his eldest brother suffered a serious loss of prestige as a direct consequence. Lindsay's litigation went nowhere and Strathearn died before effecting recovery of Urquhart, which remained firmly within the Wolf's grip. The death of his half-brother strengthened Buchan's position. The vulnerability of the north-east to Highland raids made it essential that a single strong hand should exercise royal power in the region, however dubious the methods. Buchan's survival with his offices intact was due, in no small part, to the fact there was no one to take his place.

From 1385 Carrick was also distracted by the renewal of hostilities with England and was not, therefore, in any position to interfere. In 1388 the second Earl of Douglas and Mar was killed on the field of Otterburn, but his posthumous victory confirmed Scottish military ascendancy on the borders; this was to hold until the disaster at Homildon fourteen years later.

The years of the Carrick lieutenancy saw the Wolf at the height of his power; no protest could dislodge him. Matters changed with the appointment of Fife, and this was clearly something Buchan resented. The confirmation of his brother's guardianship in May 1390 sparked a savage outburst. Forres was the first target to be given to the flames, followed on 17 June by Elgin; the perpetrators, as described by Wyntoun, were 'wyld, wikkit heland men' – the earl's cateran mercenaries.[21]

A particular target of the Wolf's wrath was the bishop of Moray, Alexander Bur. At the time of the disturbances, John Dunbar, the Earl of Moray, and Lindsay of Glen Esk were both absent in England. Bur had tried to place certain Church estates in Badenoch and Strathspey under Moray's protection, ostensibly to shield them from the Wolf's excesses, and he may have encouraged Euphemia of Ross to seek a divorce from her disagreeable consort. These attacks, savage as they were, constituted more then mere opportunistic brigandage; Buchan was attacking his brother Fife's measures, enacted in the north since 1388, and offering a demonstration that the only real power in the region was his. Perhaps he believed Carrick, as king, would also have little sympathy for the middle brother's meddling.

If so, he was mistaken; his freebooting caterans were not likely to divert so focused a mind as Fife's. Through the summer of 1390 matters did appear unstable; Robert II remained unburied and his son uncrowned.[22] Bishop Bur riposted by excommunicating his tormentor, but this sentence was revoked sometime shortly afterward, possibly during or before the coronation ceremonies at Scone by Walter Trail, bishop of St Andrews, in the presence of the king and the assembled peerage. Fife's position as Guardian remained unchallenged and Murdoch was appointed as justiciar north of the Forth – a significant check for Buchan, who must have come to terms prior to the coronation, with due compensation to Bishop Bur being agreed. Fife was not the man to tolerate such open defiance of his position and it was time to strip the Wolf of his claws.

The Guardian's first move was to repossess Castle Urquhart, where one Thomas Chisholm was installed as castellan in October 1391, an appointment he held directly from the Crown. The reversionary interest in the fortress had passed to David of Strathearn's beneficiary, his daughter Euphemia Stewart, and Fife's action may ostensibly have been on her behalf. Buchan clearly saw which way the wind was blowing and, in the following month, made one of his rare court appearances, doubtless seeking support from the king to bolster his position. In this he was disappointed.

Fife next set his sights on Ross. Buchan's abuses had steeled the countess to open proceedings against him for recovery of her estates in 1389. In this she was encouraged by her son, Alexander Leslie, who was not prepared to wait for his reviled stepfather to die before coming into his inheritance. In 1392 a trio of leading clergymen, the bishops of St Andrews, Glasgow and Aberdeen, were empowered by papal mandate to agree the divorce and the return of the countess's estate. In this the Guardian's hand may clearly be discerned; he had every incentive to support the Leslie faction, since Alexander had married Fife's daughter Isobel! Buchan's influence in Ross was, to all intents and purposes, destroyed.

Buchan vented his spleen in typical manner, dispatching his son Duncan with one of his brothers in January 1392 to harry Angus, the lands of Sir David Lindsay their target. Their cateran forces were drawn from Clan Donald and the Athollmen. Lindsay, the sheriff of Angus and Sir Patrick Gray intercepted the raiders as they were returning at Glasclune in Glenisla. After a stiff fight the Lowlanders were sorely worsted. Both Lindsay and Gray were wounded; the sheriff, Ogilvy, and his half-brother Walter Lichton were counted among the dead. Though the raid might count as a military success it was politically unsound, identifying Buchan with the very type of 'Wild' Scots the Lowlanders feared and despised. Such an act more than justified the earl's exclusion from government.

Consequently, the Council deplored his actions and outlawed both of his sons for their part in the sheriff's death, classifying them and their cateran allies as 'evil doers'.[23] Buchan was effectively marginalised and his grip on the north, if not completely broken, radically curtailed. Having dealt with his brother, Fife was soon to find himself confronted with a new rival; this time it was to be his nephew David, Earl of Carrick, the king's eldest son and heir.

Carrick was supported by his mother, Queen Annabella, and the king's generous grants of heritable pensions or annuities throughout the 1390s could be viewed as an attempt to build up a new affinity, such as he had created in the previous decade with the Lindsay/Douglas factions. Carrick entered into his earldom in early 1392 and was immediately granted a handsome annuity of £640 from customs revenues. This revitalised affinity would be concentrated south of the Forth and in the Lothians, to offset Fife's gains in the west and north. Although Fife appeared inexpugnable, his position could never be completely secure. Carrick was only twelve years of age in 1390 but a mere three years later he was introduced into the government. Fife's role was that of Guardian and so, by its very nature, finite.

By 1393 the current Anglo-Scottish truce was holding, with no sign of any immediate resumption of hostilities, and the continuance of the peace enabled Robert III to resume the reins of power, though the political running was essentially being made by Carrick and his affinity. Lawlessness was still rife in the north, however. In 1395 Sir Robert Keith laid siege to the castle of Fyvie, held by his aunt, Lady Lindsay, whom he proposed to abduct. This formed an element in a dispute between Keith and Sir James Lindsay; the former was of Fife's affinity, the latter a leading light of Carrick's party. Matters reached a bloody dénouement when Lindsay led 400 of his retainers to the lady's relief. Keith raised the siege to give battle at Bourtie in the Garioch, where he was seen off with considerable loss, leaving sixty-odd of his men breathless on the field.[24]

At Michaelmas 1396 a singular contest took place on the North Inch of Perth. It was reminiscent of the gladiatorial spectacles in Rome at their height and, more recently, the celebrated Combat of the Thirty in Brittany, where the members of rival English and French garrisons relieved the tedium of the truce by a murderous tourney. The combatants in the present case were formed by thirty champions from two contending affinities, Clan Kay and Clan Chattan. The contest had been brokered by Moray and David Lindsay as an attempt to stamp out the feud between the two by means of some wholesome communal bloodletting. An arena was constructed with seats for the spectators, which included the king and court.[25]

At the last minute one of Clan Kay came to his senses and bolted. For a difficult moment it looked as though the day's sport was spoiled. An impecunious young apprentice from Perth, with no affinity to either name, was bribed to replace the poltroon and the combat commenced in deadly earnest. Bows and blades only were allowed and the spectators were not disappointed. Of Clan Kay, only the townsman survived, while all but eleven of Clan Chattan perished. Whether this judicial slaughter achieved any lasting result is open to question, but Bower contended the north was quieter thereafter![26]

Two years later Carrick was twenty and his father created him Duke of Rothesay; at the same time Fife was elevated to his own dukedom.

Prising the reins of power finally away from Albany proved more problematic, but in 1399 Rothesay was made lieutenant on similar terms to his uncle, the appointment subject to similar constitutional checks and balances and limited to a term of three years. The grant could only be renewed thereafter on the authority of the Council, which decreed:

> sen it is welesene and kennyt that our lorde the kyng for seknes of his persoun may nocht travail to governe the Realme na restreygne trespassours and rebellours. It is sene to the consail maste expedient that the duc of Rothesay be the kyngis lieutenande generally throch al the kynrike for the terme of thre yher hafande fwl power and commissioun of the kyng to governe the lande in althyng as the kyng sulde do in his persoun gife he warr present.[27]

Rothesay's tenure was not a success; the young man had the unhappy gift of creating enemies at every turn and his mercurial temperament was given full rein when his mother died. He was initially betrothed to yet another Euphemia, the daughter of Sir William Lindsay of Rossie, but the match was deemed unsuitable for the heir to the throne. Next into the ring was the Earl of March, who offered Robert III a hefty inducement to accept his daughter, Elizabeth Dunbar. Douglas cannily pipped March at the post, by offering a still larger incentive and seeing off the Dunbar proposal on the grounds that the match had not been approved by Parliament. In the end, it was Marjorie Douglas who won the race and March, infuriated by what he perceived as collusion between Douglas and Rothesay, left the realm to offer his capable sword to the English.

Events in England had reached a crisis in 1399, when John of Gaunt's exiled heir, Henry Bolingbroke, returned to England to demand his unjustly confiscated estates from Richard II. The king had unwisely seized on the vast Lancastrian inheritance as a ready means of easing his own financial pressures. Richard was in Ireland when the storm broke and failed to rally support. The Lancastrian Bolingbroke usurped the throne as Henry IV and Richard died soon afterward in captivity.

Robert III refused to recognise the new king of England and persisted in referring to him in correspondence as 'Duke of Lancaster, Earl of Derby and Steward of England'. Such condescension was dangerous; the Percies had supported the usurper and had already benefited, and the presence of an experienced commander such as March in the enemy ranks was a dangerous development. Douglas and the other hawks were more than ready for war and a renewal of hostilities seemed imminent.

Rothesay's appointment brought the Drummond faction back to the fringes of power. The queen was vociferous in her complaints against Albany and his administration, mainly concerning her arrears of pension. The young duke had a committee of twenty advisors to ease him into the role of government, but the plain fact was he remained totally unsuited to the role. So great were his excesses that Albany finally persuaded the king, who had hitherto rested all his hopes on his eldest son, to abandon him. It is difficult not to feel sympathy for the broken old man, the prey of these competing factions, himself temperamentally affected, half disabled, and with his final carefully-wrought hopes dashed.

In January 1402 Albany struck, having persuaded a vacillating King Robert to abandon his son. Rothesay was arrested and incarcerated in the duke's castle of Falkland. By 25 March he was dead, ostensibly of natural causes. It was said he died from dysentery, or that he was weakened by starvation. A writer from the mid-fifteenth century recounts this version of events:

> Wherfor the lordes the nobles of the reaume of Scotlande, considering that vicious living of that saide Duke of Rothesay and soore dreiding yf he hadde reynede afther hys fader that many inconveniences misfortunes and vengeances might have followed and fallen uppon al that region by cause of his lyff soo openly knowen vicious, shortly the advyse takyne and full purpoisse of the great lordes of that lande and in especialte by the myghtie and the favourable puissance of the Duke of Albanie and of therlle Douglas the saide Duke of Rossaye maugre al his helpers by forsce was taken and emprisoned within the castel of Fflakland that by duress of samyn hee eate his awne handes and died in grete distresse and myserie, the whiche was against goddes lawe and manes lawe and pittie to think that such unrighteous malice should be doone to any prince whatsoever he be.[28]

The duke was buried in the neighbouring abbey of Lindores; his no doubt grieving father endowed a chaplaincy in the parish church of Dundee in his memory. The queen had died the previous year, as had another of Rothesay's principal supporters, the bishop of St Andrews, and the old Earl of Douglas. The subsequent enquiry, presumably to no one's surprise, cleared his uncle of any complicity in his death. Sir Malcolm Drummond, another of Rothesay's partisans, was effectively kidnapped from his castle of Kildrummy and died shortly thereafter. Such convenience naturally raised fresh suspicions.

Albany was now firmly back in control, but was equally in the sway of the war party led by Archibald Douglas. A pretender to the English throne, claiming to be Richard II, had been discovered in the unlikely haven of the Lord of the Isles's kitchen. This individual, known as the 'Mammet' (scarecrow), was best described as a 'half witted scullion', but was nonetheless adopted by the Crown as the real Richard and ended his days as a royal pensioner in Stirling.

The new Earl of Douglas was the architect of the disastrous invasion of Northumberland in 1402. The host he commanded was a national army, perhaps 10,000-strong. Having harried the county, the invaders found their escape blocked near Wooler by a force led by Hotspur and March. The ensuing fight, in which Douglas displayed a lamentable lack of generalship (he was thereafter known as the 'Tineman' or loser, an unhelpful sobriquet for a commander), was a wholly one-sided slaughter. Ably guided by March, Hotspur let his Welsh and Cheshire archers do the work, shooting down the passive schiltroms until they broke and tried to flee. Hundreds were cut down and more drowned. Albany's son and heir, Murdoch, was among the haul of captives.

The new heir to the throne, James, was only eight and, even if the king was prepared to accept that Albany had not murdered his eldest son, he proposed to take no chances with the younger. The boy would be sent to France; the perils of the sea crossing and English privateers were deemed less than the peril of continued proximity to his powerful uncle. The embarkation would be from an east-coast port away from the duke's strongholds of Dundonald and Rothesay. In February 1406 the king's trusted counsellor, Sir David Fleming, was burdened with the difficult task of conveying the boy, under strong escort, to North Berwick and from there, by ship's boat, to the Bass Rock where he would take ship for France.

That part of the mission went smoothly, but during his return journey on 14 February Fleming was ambushed by a substantial force under the joint command of James Douglas of Balvany, Alexander Seton of Gordon and William St Clair of Herdsmanston. In the fight which ensued, Fleming was killed. The fracas probably stemmed from Douglas's anger that the dead knight had warned the English fugitives, Northumberland and Lord Bardolph, to flee before they could be taken and exchanged for the Tineman and Murdoch.

In the culminating tragedy of Robert III's life, James never reached France. His vessel was intercepted, in flagrant violation of the truce by English privateers, and the boy sent as a royal captive to the king. For the next eighteen years James I would remain a pawn of the English Crown while Albany enjoyed an extended tenure as regent. This final blow hastened the old king's miserable demise and the Albany Stewarts fully came into their own.

3

The Lordship of the Isles

The reapers sing of war,
War with the shining wing;
The minstrels sing of war,
Of winged war.

The Gododdin[1]

Men of might in battle eager,
Boast of burning Njal's abode.
Have the princes heard how sturdy
Seahorse raiders sought revenge?
Hath not since, on foemen holding
High the shield's broad orb aloft,
All that wrong been fully wroken?
Raw flesh ravens got to tear.

Saga of Burnt Njal[2]

If you are driving southward on the present A816 heading from Oban and passing the southern tip of Loch Awe, through Kilmichael and Kilmartin, then you will find yourself in an enchanted landscape where traces of our distant past abound. Rising from the plain, on the right just before you reach the churchyard at Kilmachumaig, is the great hill fort of Dunadd. This mighty rock-hewn fortress was the capital of Dalriada ('Riada's Portion'). For centuries it dominated the landscape and withstood the attacks of hostile Picts. In 736 their warlike king, Tallorcan, defeated Muiredach of Dalriada at the battle of Cnoc Coirpri, which may have been fought toward the shores of Loch Awe at what is now Ederline (identified with the supposed location of the fight at Etar Lindu: 'between two pools'). In the aftermath, the Pictish king's brother Angus successfully stormed Dunadd.

A stiff scramble up the conical mound brings you to the twin plateaux that comprise the summit. On the narrow spur between the two lies the 'Inauguration Stone', the outline of a human foot incised into the rock. Nearby is a shallow basin cut from the stone and the relief of a boar. It was here that the ancient kings were consecrated, each one slipping his shoeless foot into the carving, a symbolic affirmation that the new king would follow the ways of his forbears.

The exact function of the boar is unclear, though it is most likely the basin was used for ritual ablutions as part of the ceremony. With fine views along Kilmartin Glen and the serpentine trail of the river Add, the whole place resonates with the pull of history. The citadel echoes the cyclopean masonry of the Bronze Age settlements from Homeric Greece, Mycenae, Tiryns and Argos.

In 258 AD the Irish warlord Cairbre Riada, son of the High King Conar, who already held a province of Dalriada in Ulster, landed on the coast of Argyll and established a principality there. This was probably a fairly modest foothold and the kingdom did not begin to take shape until after 500 AD, when fresh waves of immigrants crossed the narrow sea under Fergus mac Erc. They established their capital at Dunadd ('the fort of the river Add'), on the plain of Moine Mhor and, for several centuries, became involved in near-endemic warfare with their neighbours the Picts to the east and the Strathclyde Britons to the south. The Romans had described these Irish Celts from Antrim as *Scoti*, later 'the Scots', and when their chief Kenneth MacAlpin united the Picts and Scots into a single nation in the ninth century they gave their name to the whole.

Toward the end of that same century the Norsemen launched the first of what was to be a continuous pattern of raids, their sleek-oared galleys perfectly adapted to sweeping undetected up the long sea lochs. The relatively unsophisticated Hebridean craft of the day were no match for these sturdy clinker-built vessels. In the words of the early-tenth-century chronicler of the Norse impact on Ireland:

There were countless sea vomitings of ships and boats. Not one harbour or landing port or fortress in all of Munster was without fleets of Danes and pirates. There came the fleet of Oiberd and the fleet of Oduinn and the fleets of Griffin, Snatgar, Lagmann, Erolf, Sitruic, Buidnin, Birndin, Liagrislach, Toirberdach, Eoan Barun, Milid Buu, Suimin, Suainin and lastly the fleet of the Inghen Ruaidh. All the evil Ireland had so far suffered was as nothing compared to the evil inflicted by these men. The whole of Munster was plundered. They built fortresses and landing ports all over Ireland. They made spoil land and sword land. They ravaged Ireland's churches and sanctuaries and destroyed her reliquaries and books. They killed Ireland's kings and chieftains and champion warriors. They enslaved our blooming, lively women, taking them over the broad green sea.[3]

Forays gave way to colonisation and the whole of the western seaboard and the islands were, by the tenth century, dotted with permanent Norse settlements. The Vikings were never truly conquerors in the imperial sense. They intermarried with the indigenous population to form a mixed race of Norse Gaels; in time they took the cross and blended into the rich tapestry of the developing landscape.

The great chieftain and war leader Somerled mac Gillebride, from whom the Lords of the Isles were to claim their descent, was of mixed Norse Gael ancestry and could, it was alleged, trace his line back through the kings of Dalriada to the second-century Irish paladin Conn of the Hundred Battles. His grandfather Gilladomnan and father Gillebride both married into the Norse nobility and held sway over areas of Argyll and the Isles. Their tenure was rudely interrupted in 1098 when the king of Norway, Magnus Bareleg,[4] descended in force to remind his Norse Gael subjects of their true loyalties. Both Gilladomnan and his son found their semi-independent status quashed and they and their families were reduced to skulking in the heather before fleeing to Ireland.

Somerled, or Sumarlidi,[5] was thus born in exile and grew to early manhood in Fermanagh and Monaghan, held by the Macmahons and Maguires. He was baptised into the Christian faith but his education was primarily martial, about how to fight well on both land and sea. The Norse had won their many victories not only because their ships were better but because their fighting skills were superbly honed, their weapons and harness were more plentiful, and they could demonstrate high levels of discipline:

Not one of the champions of the Irish was able to deliver us from the tyranny of these foreign hordes. This is because of the excellence of the foreigners' polished, treble-plaited, heavy coats of mail, their hard, strong swords, their well-rivetted long spears, and because of the greatness of their bravery and ferocity and their hunger for the pure, sweet grassland of Ireland.[6]

The Norse Gaels received a respite when, in 1103, Magnus Bareleg made his final foray into Ireland and was killed in ambush. In the course of the next couple of decades Gillebride and his affinity fought, largely without success, to recover their former domain in Ardnamurchan and Morvern. Some of the bruised survivors returned empty-handed back to Ireland, while the displaced chieftain and his son skulked around Loch Linnhe.

Despite the lack of any tangible gains, the young Somerled had clearly made an impression as a warrior. When a chief of Clan MacInnes died, his kin elected the Norse Gael prince as his successor. Now with a viable base in Morvern and a swollen warband, Somerled made his presence felt in Argyll, subduing the Norse and taking their galleys as prizes. The captured ships formed the nucleus of his war fleet and he harnessed sea power to gain control of Lorn, Knapdale and Kintyre.

The wild and lovely landscapes of the Ardnamurchan peninsula still bear the names of Somerled's victories: Ath Tharacaill (Acharacle), the Ford of Torquil, where the Viking fell beneath his blade, and Glenborrowdale, where another Norseman, Borodil, was slain.[7] In 1140 the now well-established ruler cemented an important alliance when he married Ragnhild, the daughter of Olaf, King of Man. This vibrant Norse outpost was virtually an independent principality and Olaf, secure behind the wooden walls of his navy, ruled for over forty years.

The dynasty of Man had been founded in the preceding century by a Norse freebooter of the old school, Godred Crovan, who had stood behind the doomed shield wall at Stamford Bridge with Harald Hardradi. Escaping the rout, he had taken Man and was established there in 1079, extending his grip into the Isles before dying in 1095. It had been the power and independence of Man that had influenced King Magnus's decision to exert his authority.[8] His son Lagman was succeeded by a younger son, Olaf – the same king, described as of small stature but exceedingly able,[9] whose daughter was now to marry Somerled.

Somerled had not been previously married, although he appears to have enjoyed the caresses of a number of concubines, one of whom gave him a son, Gillecolm. Ragnhild, in turn, bore him three further sons: Dugall, Ranald and Angus. From the loins of the first two sprang the clans of Dougall, Donald and Ruari. Their daughter Bethoc achieved the distinction of becoming abbess of the Augustinian nunnery on Iona. In the thirteen years from the date of his marriage alliance until the death of David I of Scotland in 1153, Somerled cannily steered a careful course in the maelstrom of Norse and Scottish politics, while steadily increasing his influence through an expanding fleet and a swelling array of spears.

David I was not the only royal casualty of that year. On Man, Olaf was bloodily assassinated by his Irish nephews, while the young king of Scots, Malcolm IV, allowed the continued steady immigration of land-hungry Normans begun by his predecessor. Olaf's determined son, Godred Du ('Godred the Black'), returned from Norway via Orkney and wreaked a savage revenge on his father's killers, pursuing the survivors back into Ireland and winning both fame and spoil. These successes, however, bred a fatal arrogance and contempt for his neighbours which led Godred to alienate most of his contemporaries. So intense was the hatred his tyrannies generated that a confederation of the chiefs, led by Torfinn Ottarson, who himself had aspirations to the throne in Dublin, petitioned Somerled's son Dugall to lead an attempt to unseat his reviled uncle.

Godred reacted swiftly, despatching his sleek-hulled galleys across the cold waters in January 1156. An epic sea battle was fought out beneath the stark winter's moon at Caol Isla in the Sound of Islay on the Feast of the Epiphany.[10] Birlinns and nyvaigs clashed and collided; the naval tactics of the day might see the defending side rope several boats together with those having the highest shipboards on the outside of the array. This then provided an arena for the clash of spears – a land battle fought at sea, the decks soon slippery with blood. The attackers would lay alongside and attempt to board. The birlinns, being smaller and handier, would bicker on the fringes, as skirmishers would deploy on land.[11] The Manxmen had heavier ships and probably more of them, but could make no headway against the Islesmen. Somerled and Dugall fought Godred to a standstill.

If the battle was technically a draw, Godfred's fangs had been blunted, and he was obliged to cede the islands south of Ardnamurchan to buy a truce. Two years later Somerled mounted an amphibious assault on Man with fifty-odd ships. This time there was no margin of doubt; Godred was decisively thrashed off Ramsey and obliged to flee back to Norway, where he flung himself on the mercy of King Inge.

Somerled, styling himself *Rex Insularum* ('King of the Isles'), was at the very height of his power. He and his sons held sway over some 25,000 square miles of territory, both on the mainland and in a wide necklace of over 500 islands stretching from the Butt of Lewis to the Calf of Man. All of these scattered holdings were united by the broad highway of the Atlantic and the Irish Sea where the Islesmen now ruled unchallenged.

Somerled's galleys were sustained by a network of forts providing secure anchorages in the seal lochs and islands. A good example is Dunyvaig ('the Fort of the Nyvaigs'), located on the strategically important south-ern tip of the Sound of Islay.[12] The island itself became, from time to time, the focus of Somerled's lordship, the scene of Council meetings, feasting, games and the bards who sang of wars and warriors.[13] In the later medieval period many of the castles of the Highlands – Mingary, Aros, Ardtornish, Duart and Tioram – were rebuilt over the foundations of these early forts. Sween in Knapdale and Skipness by Kintyre also owe their beginnings to this period.

By 1160 Somerled's grip seemed unshakeable, but the more southerly of his domains, Argyll, Lorn, Knapdale, Kintyre and the scattering of islands in the Clyde estuary, were at risk from royal aggression. The King of the Isles had earlier, and perhaps unwisely, supported his brother-in-law Malcolm MacHeth in an abortive bid to wrest the crown from David I. Malcolm's son Donald had since raised his banners against Malcolm IV. Both father and son now languished in Roxburgh. David had demanded knight service of the men of Lorn and the Isles to support his attempt to extend the southern boundaries of the kingdom as far as the Tweed. The king of Scots and his host were confronted and badly mauled by the northern English gentry at Northallerton; the unprotected Islesmen and Gallowegians suffered heavy losses.

Malcolm IV had little respect for the Gael but was canny enough to complete the marginalisation of the MacHeths by concluding separate terms with both Somerled and Fergus of Galloway. When Fergus died in 1161, the king allowed his expansionist Norman knights licence to spread their influence into lands historically controlled solely by Gaels. One of the most ambitious of these routiers was Walter Fitzalan, who began the process of feudalisation by raising a motte and a civilian settlement near Inchinnan, at the confluence of the Cart and Clyde. These works were a dagger aimed at the heart of Somerled's lordship, and the earlier challenge from Godred seemed puny by comparison.

He laid his plans with care; the challenge was too blatant to be ignored and must be met with force. Somerled did not, however, underestimate the fighting prowess of these Norman knights, sprung from the same virile stock as his own Norse ancestors. Like a medieval Agamemnon, for three years he summoned, bribed, entreated and cajoled, in order to build a formidable coalition. In the end, by 1164 he could count upon some 4,000 broadswords, a mighty host with Norse Gaels from Argyll, Kintyre, Ireland and the Isles. The army mustered on the lower Clyde and the fleet took them around Greenock to make landfall toward Renfrew and Inchinnan.

The Norman's land and holdings were thoroughly wasted; his people despoiled, slain or displaced. The host splashed through the shallows of the Cart to launch an assault on the invader's timber bastion. From the palisade and tower, defiant shafts thudded into the attackers' ranks. Undeterred by the fearsome odds, Fitzalan's mailed knights charged home time and again, riding stirrup to stirrup, pennons fluttering and lances spitting.

The advance was met, stalled and repulsed. At this time the lance was not necessarily held couched under the arm but, being lighter than the later and much heavier knightly lance, could be used overarm as a spear or even as a missile; in fact, Somerled is said to have been felled by a thrown lance. The Gaels, clinging to the foot deployment of the Norsemen, were simply no match for heavy cavalry. Lowland foot from Glasgow came up, setting fire to the heather to mask their paucity of numbers. More importantly, Fitzalan was reinforced by additional heavy horse and went onto the offensive.

The King of the Isles died sword in hand. His son Gillecolm also fell, possibly trying to cover the host's withdrawal, which became disordered and finally, beset by the relentless pressure from the seemingly tireless Normans, dissolved into rout. The fleeing men, all thoughts of glory forgotten, struggled to escape back to the boats. Many were spitted as they ran; others drowned in the press.

The horror of the slaughter is caught by the author of the *Carmen de Morte Sumerlidi*:

Here a marvel. To the terrible, the battle was terrible. Heather and furze bushes moving their heads; burnt thyme and branches; brambles and ferns, caused panic, appearing to the enemy as soldiers. Never in this life had such miracles been heard. Shadows of thyme and ordure [smoke] were bulwarks of defense. And in the first cleft of battle the baleful leader fell. Wounded by a javelin, slain by the sword, Somerled died. And the raging wave swallowed his son, and the wounded of many thousand fugitives; because when this fierce leader was struck down, the wicked took to flight; and very many were slaughtered, both on sea and on land.[14]

The first military clash between Gael and Teuton had ended in a decisive and unequivocal victory for the latter. An army of footsoldiers could not mount an attack on a strongly fortified position while seeking to resist cavalry. The battle of Hastings, in 1066, had amply demonstrated the superiority of the mailed and mounted knight over the footsoldier. The Norse Gael had now experienced the same bitter and bloody lesson as the southern English.

Despite the signal triumph Fitzalan had won and the interregnum following Somerled's death, the Crown made no attempt to follow up the victory. This was probably due to the lack of a fleet rather than an absence of will, but it may have been about now that Fitzalan gained a foothold in Bute; the family were certainly established there by 1200. Malcolm IV himself died in the following year, to be succeeded by his brother, William the Lion. The indefatigable Godred, returning from exile, seized the moment to claw back his kingdom of Man.

The King of the Isles left his three sons by Ragnhild living at his death and their sprawling patrimony was, in the Celtic manner, divided between them. Dugall, the eldest, received Argyll with Mull, Coll and Tiree. Ranald was awarded Islay, Jura and Kintyre. Angus, the youngest, appears to have taken the lands west of Ardnamurchan and around Moidart on the mainland, with possibly Rhum, Eigg, Bute (if not already occupied by Fitzalan), Arran and Skye.

After a Celtic division there was a Celtic civil war. Ranald, grandly styling himself as 'King of the Isles, Lord of Argyll and Kintyre', went to war with his elder brother over possession of Mull. At the same time he fought with Angus who, in 1192, defeated him. The youngest brother, together with his three sons, was cut down eighteen years later in a fight with the men of Skye and probably those of Man, whose Norse dynasty had long laid claim to the island. On Angus's death his claim to Bute passed finally to the Stewarts; his granddaughter was married to Alexander Fitzalan and the rump of his lands was parcelled out between his brothers.

Little more is known of the middle brother, Ranald; he may have perished in the battle against Angus or he may have lived on for a number of years, dying as late as 1221. From the time of Somerled's sons, known collectively as the MacSorleys, we begin to detect the emergence of patronymics. Those who followed Dugall came to be the Macdougalls; Ranald's successors became Macdonalds and Macruaris. One of his sons, Donald, took Islay and his brother, Ruari, got lands in Moidart and the northern Isles.

Of Donald, again, little concrete evidence emerges, save that the dynasty he founded was a lasting one. It is possible that the MacSorleys collectively had strained relations with the Crown. The closing years of the reign of William the Lion and the earlier days of Alexander II were marked by disturbances surrounding various Celtic pretenders. These were sufficiently troublesome for Alexander to incur the expense of fitting out expeditions to the Isles in 1221 and again in the following year. Both of these *chevauchées* were supported by a naval arm.

Ruari was apparently driven out of Kintyre and his holding there enfeoffed to Donald, which suggests the former had been lending support to the challengers. Alexander proceeded to consolidate his authority by beginning construction of a new burgh at Dumbarton. The Stewarts were expanding also, into Cowal, and erected a new motte at Dunoon.

About this time the King of Norway, Hakon IV, began making noises and found it expedient to remind Alexander II of the terms of the earlier accord of 1098, which had reaffirmed Norwegian interests in the west and the islands. His initial expedition of 1230 was captained by a warrior named Uspak, who may have been another son of Dugall MacSorley. The Norse struck at Bute in obvious resentment of the Norman dominance.

King Alexander then offered to either redraft the terms of the treaty of 1098 or, as he would prefer, to buy the Norwegians out altogether. Neither alternative appealed to Hakon, who upped the stakes by appointing his nominee Ewan Macdougall as 'King' of the Isles. This Macdougall, though of Celtic descent, was also a leading feudal magnate in Argyll, and in 1249 Alexander mounted a further expedition into the west to remind Ewan of his proper allegiance, but died suddenly on Kerrera before fully accomplishing his objective.

The contentious question of sovereignty lapsed during the minority of Alexander III, but it was not a matter that could be expected simply to go away. The burgeoning power of the Scottish kings and the development of a viable feudal state inevitably implied that the days of Norse rule were, at best, numbered. The kings of Norway simply did not have the logistical capability to resist their Scottish counterparts.

It is not possible to pinpoint exactly the year of Donald of Islay's death but it may have been in or around 1250. He was followed by his energetic son, Angus Mor, who early in his career was militarily active in Ireland, harrying the English there. So troublesome was he that an ordinance of 1256 specifically barred his presence in the land for a term of seven years.[15] His freebooting style sufficed to earn him the respect and approbation of his Celtic contemporaries and he became the first chief of Clan Donald to be honoured in verse:

> Though he came round Ireland; rare is the strand whence he has not taken cattle: graceful long ships are sailed by thee, thou are like an otter, O scion of Tara.
>
> The House of Somerled, the race of Godfried, whence thou art sprung, who did not store up cattle, O fresh planted orchard, O apple branch, noble is each blood from which thou comest.[16]

Despite this impressive Norse pedigree, Angus accepted the inevitability of Scottish power and tactfully named his eldest son Alexander (Alasdair). When the young king came into his own after 1260, he sent a further embassy to Hakon with a further cash offer. Unwisely, the Norwegian king maintained his unwilling stance and Alexander embarked on less cordial means. Man was by now impotent, and two years later the Earl of Ross seized Skye by force of arms in the name of the king. Hakon riposted in the summer of 1263 by summoning a general muster at Bergen and preparing to take the field.

If the Norwegian was expecting to repeat his predecessor's grand *chevauchée* of 1098, he was to be disappointed in the support he could muster from the Isles; only the Macruaris responded to his call. Ewan of Argyll was careful to affirm his loyalty to Alexander III. At first Angus of Islay felt constrained to fall in behind the Norwegian's banner; almost certainly this move was dictated by expediency – his lands were otherwise too exposed.

The threat of autumnal gales already hung in the chill wind as the last great Viking fleet sailed into the Clyde. The Scots were not eager for a fight; the onset of winter must soon compel the invaders to withdraw. Angus, with Dougald and Alan Macdougall and Magnus of Man all marching beneath his banner, led a commanded party into the Stewart's holdings in Lennox around Loch Lomond, a satisfying application of fire and steel. An opportunity to check the relentless ambition of these Norman incomers was not to be missed!

This was a mere diversion; the main action flared around a series of skirmishes which came to be known as the battle of Largs. The Norsemen, like Somerled, came off worst, though their actual losses were few. It is unlikely that Hakon registered the affair as a defeat. It was not Norman lances but the encroaching grip of autumn storms that decided the day. The whole expedition had been a huge bluff; once that bluff was called, the thing simply collapsed.

The Scots won decisively because the failure of the expedition showed quite plainly that the Norwegians, remote at Bergen, could not impose their will on the Isles in the face of sustained opposition from the king of Scots. Hakon never regained his kingdom, dying in Orkney in December, and as he breathed his last the remaining vestiges of the Viking age passed with him.

Alexander was quick to capitalise on his advantage. The following summer he brought the MacSorleys and Magnus of Man to heel; both were only too ready to submit. When the Manx king died in 1265, his lands passed to the Scottish Crown. It was only Dugald Macruari who stood by his Norse allegiance and maintained defiance until he died in 1268.

His stand was anachronistic; Hakon's successor, another Magnus, accepted the inevitable and, by the Treaty of Perth, sealed in July 1266, Norway ceded all of the Western Isles to Scotland. Alexander could afford a show of magnanimity, and all those who had nailed their banners to the Norwegian standard were given a full amnesty.

With the matter of sovereignty finally decided, the MacSorleys took their place in the councils of the Scottish polity along with the other magnates. Angus Macdonald, Alexander Macdougall and Alan Macruari all attended the meeting of the Great Council summoned at Scone, in 1284, to debate the hiatus in the succession arising from the death of the king's heir.[17] The MacSorleys agreed with the rest to the nomination of the Maid of Norway (the granddaughter of Alexander III, whose daughter had married King Magnus). This was a clear divergence from Celtic practice and an acceptance of the rule of primogeniture.[18]

In 1286 Alexander III, still in his prime, hurrying through foul weather to receive the embraces of his young Queen Yolande of Dreux and determined to honour his obligation to father more sons, fell to his death on a wild and windy night. His broken body was not found by the searchers until the next morning. The king's sudden and tragic death ushered in an interregnum which, after the early death of his infant heir, eventually led to the choosing of John Balliol and the agonies that followed. Quite soon after the king's death, Angus of Islay entered into an accord with Bruce the Competitor and James Stewart, referred to as the Turnberry Band. This agreement ostensibly referred to matters in Ireland but was, in reality, a manifesto for the Bruce faction.

Clan Dougall were already related to the Comyns, who were to support Balliol and who, in due course, became mortal enemies of Bruce. This enmity reached its violent dénouement in 1306 when Bruce and his affinity murdered the 'Red' Comyn on sacred ground in Dumfries. Long before that, the Parliament summoned by King John in 1292 was ready to reward his supporters. Alexander Macdougall was granted the important post of sheriff of Lorn, making him the Crown's principal agent in the west.

Angus of Islay did not appear, neither did his eldest son and heir, Alexander. The spectre of internecine strife now stalking the realm was matched by mounting tension between the MacSorleys, who were bitterly divided over an acrimonious land dispute.

This contention had arisen over the marriage portion of Juliana Macdougall, a daughter or perhaps sister of the Lord of Argyll, which was supposed to include possession of the island of Lismore. One of the more humiliating aspects of John Balliol's submission to Longshanks was that litigants had the right of appeal to the courts in England, and this matter came before the King's Bench in 1292. The sovereign bound both Angus and Alexander to keep the peace, implying that some disturbances may already have occurred. The case dragged on at least until 1295 and it seems the king was minded to find in Macdougall's favour, though the matter was unresolved when war broke out in the following year.

Angus of Islay was already dead and Alexander had come into his estate. He had two brothers, one called Angus and a younger sibling,

Iain, known as *sprangaich* ('the bold').[19] Alexander had already bested
Campbell of Lochawe in battle, when he swore fealty to Longshanks.
The king did not repose any great trust in him. Briefly incarcerated after
the fall of Berwick, he was at liberty the following year – the heady summer of the Wallace/Murray rebellion and the humiliation of the English
at Stirling Bridge.

That notwithstanding, it would be too simplistic to brand Alexander
as a patriot. Nationalist sentiment was in its very infancy; men thought
primarily of loyalty to family and expediency played a significant role.
Alexander's later support for Bruce was largely opportunistic and dictated
by his enmity toward the Macdougalls, firmly placed in the Anglophile
Comyn faction.

In the wake of Wallace's disastrous defeat at Falkirk, the Macdougalls,
supported by the wild Macruaris, stepped up the pressure on Alexander,
who was constrained to write to Edward requesting he instruct the
magnates of Argyll and Ross to maintain some semblance of law and
order. The murder of John Comyn in 1306 propelled the remnants of
the Balliol faction firmly into the English camp. Wallace had fought
in the name of King John; the Bruce insurgency introduced an internecine element, a state of civil war between the Balliol/Comyn faction
and the Bruce party. It has been suggested that Alexander of Islay was
captured, perhaps in the rout of Methven or thereafter, and died in gaol
in 1308. However, an entry in the Ulster Annals reveals his death in combat against Alexander Macdougall in January 1299.

Alexander submitted to Longshanks in 1305, by which time, following the siege of Stirling, the English king had finally achieved 'an end
to the business'. The patriot cause in Scotland appeared to be utterly
spent. Wallace the paladin had died a ghastly traitor's death and the magnates had bowed to the seemingly inevitable. Until Bruce so noticeably
unfurled his banner the following year, it appeared that the realm was
entirely subjugated.

The killing of the Red Comyn had a momentous effect on the
political map of the western Highlands. Alexander of Argyll's submission had secured his lands and he continued to hold onto Lismore.
At the outset, the prospects for the Bruce faction – 'King Hobbe', as
the English contemptuously dubbed him – appeared unpromising.
Although crowned king of Scots in a threadbare ceremony derided by
his queen, a daughter of the 'Red' Earl of Antrim, Bruce was trounced

by Aymer de Valence at Methven, and the battered survivors further thinned in the course of a second defeat at Dail Righ (Dalry) near Tyndrum by Argyll's son John, known as *Bacach* ('the lame').[20]

The fugitive king, apparently without prospects, skulked in the heather. He had few remaining allies, but enmity with the Macdougalls meant support from both Neil Campbell of Lochawe and, importantly, Angus Og, who had replaced his dead brother as chief in 1301. Barbour has left us this description of the chief welcoming the royal outlaw:

> Angus of Islay then was sire
> And lord and leader of Kintyre
> The king right gladly welcomed he
> And promised him his fealty
> And offered freely out of hand
> Such service as he might demand
> And for a stronghold to him gave
> Dubaverty, his castle safe,
> To dwell therein as he might need.
> Right thankfully the king agreed
> And gladly took his fealty.[21]

This was a crucial juncture; without Angus's support the Bruce cause might well not have survived that grim winter of 1306 to 1307. Edward I, feeling the inexorable tug of mortality which even his iron will could ultimately not deflect, was determined to crush this upstart whose continued survival might expose the fragility of his Scottish settlement. Dunaverty was stormed and Bruce was once more on the run, sheltering in the deep glens and scattered islands.

The death of Longshanks at Burgh on Sands on 7 July 1307 was to prove another turning point. Edward of Caernarvon was not the man his father had been – vacillating, hedonistic, obsessed with a series of catamites (initially the comely Gascon, Piers Gaveston) and frequently at odds with the great magnates of his realm. The first foray ended badly when Thomas and Alexander Bruce, attempting an amphibious assault upon Galloway, were met and defeated by Domnal Macdougall. Both of Bruce's brothers lost their lives in consequence. Another sibling, Neil, had been executed after an epic defence of Kildrummy the preceding year.

Support for the Bruce cause was no more than a trickle in these early and uncertain days. John Macdougall was relentless in his pursuit, bringing in tracker dogs while his clansmen beat the heather. There was comfort in store; Bruce turned the tables on his persecutors in a skirmish in Glentrool in April, and the next month he bested de Valence at Loudon Hill. In that summer the heart went out of the English occupation and the initiative now passed to the patriots. From this point until his death in 1329, Bruce was to remain on the offensive, and he never again lost tactical supremacy.

The weakness of the English position overall was that the series of strongpoints and garrison outposts could only be sustained by a mobile field army. Once the tactical initiative was surrendered to the patriots, the garrisons were left exposed and isolated. Bruce could concentrate his forces, however meagre at the outset, and deal with his enemies each in turn. The outposts, once taken, were for the most part slighted to remove their usefulness.

In the autumn of that year, Bruce, with his Macdonald and Macruari allies (for Christiana Macruari had joined the cause and brought more long-oared galleys and nimble kerns to the standard), broke out of the west and stormed the length of the Great Glen to confront the Comyn faction in the north-east. The taking up or 'herschip' of Buchan was fierce and thorough, despite the king's debilitating illness. Though still pitifully weak, Bruce led his tiny army to a decisive victory over the Comyns at Inverurie in May 1308.

John of Argyll, also ill and now finding himself besieged in Dunstaffnage, wrote in despairing terms to Edward II, seeking to explain why he had felt obliged to agree to a truce:

> I was confined to my bed with illness, and have been for six months past, Bruce approached these parts by land and sea with 10,000 men they say, or 15,000. I have no more than 800 men, 500 in my own pay whom I keep continually to guard the borders of my territory. The barons of Argyll give me no aid. Yet Bruce asked for a truce, which I granted him for a short space.[22]

While the king harried in the north the redoubtable Douglas, together with Edward Bruce, had thoroughly taken up Galloway, Douglas wreaking fearful revenge on the Clifford garrison. In August 1308, John of

Argyll, still unrecovered, sought to contest the patriot encroachment at the Pass of Brander. The Macdougalls were strongly placed on the slopes of steep-sided Ben Cruachan but, outflanked by Douglas and assailed from the front, they broke and by the autumn Dunstaffnage had fallen. John of Argyll sought refuge in flight and his ageing father, Alexander, who had led the last desperate defence, bent his knee to Robert Bruce. The day of the Macdougalls was over and it was not until the rise of the Campbells at the end of the century that Clan Donald would face any serious rival in the west.

Bruce summoned a Parliament to be held at St Andrews in 1309, a clear indication that his kingship had surmounted the challenge of internal rivals; the Balliol/Comyn faction were effectively played out. Angus Og did not appear to represent Clan Donald; the Islesmen sent Donald of Islay, possibly a nephew or son of the last chief, Alexander. It may even be that Angus Og was never formally elevated to the office; his role may have been more akin to that of a war leader, a *dux bellorum*.

For the next five years Bruce and his swelling affinity, including his brother Edward, the fiery Douglas and Randolph, steadily clawed back castle, town and outpost from the English in a savage, incessant guerrilla campaign of ambush and escalade. No pitched battles were fought, through policy rather than fear. Bruce wanted to recover his country a piece at a time, never striking so notable a blow as to bring down a massive reprisal, a war of outposts. Only the threat to Stirling, besieged by Edward Bruce, may have sparked the very reaction his brother had sought to avoid, a major English expedition.

On 24 and 25 June 1314 the patriots were to face their most severe test, confronted by the pride of English chivalry, a vast panoply of proud banners and mettlesome destriers. On the first day, fumbling English attempts to bypass the patriots and thus effect a technical relief of the castle were easily rebuffed, the schiltroms standing fast against the heavy horse of Clifford and de Beaumont, who were obliged to retire in some disorder. A frontal attack was easily seen off, and in the luminescent dawn of the next morning the Scots prepared to assume the offensive; this was to be the deciding moment.

The king, who had mightily impressed his Highland subjects when he so neatly despatched De Bohun on the first day, now gave Angus Og command of the reserve, comprised mainly of Gaels.

Their moment came at the very crisis of the fight, when Bruce committed them on the right to support his brother's hard-pressed brigade. On that day Clan Donald fought for king and country and gave good service, such good service that it is said Bruce, in recognition of the valour of the Islesmen, decreed that Macdonald should thereafter always hold the right of the line. This may be apocryphal, but the tradition survived as long as the clan's final charge on Drummossie Moor on a foul April day in 1746.

With the humbling of Edward II at Bannockburn, Scotland was not only free of the invader's presence but able to assume the military initiative and carry the fight into northern England. The battle was a key point in the War of Independence, but it did not bring about a cessation of hostilities. Thereafter until the conclusion of the Treaty of Northampton, Bruce carried the war to the English, a savage business of foray and destruction, leavened with blackmail. The strategic aim was to force Edward to recognise Bruce as a free prince and to formally abandon claims of sovereignty. The tactics were fire, sword and extortion.

In this the Highlanders were very much in their element; they could march fast, strike hard and live off the land. The warbands that so ruthlessly harried the northern counties of England from 1314 were comprised of highly mobile mounted infantry or light cavalry; they marched without a straggling logistical tail and were entirely self-sufficient. Clan Donald fought in the extended skirmish at Old Byland when King Edward was nearly taken, swarming up the steep flank of the English position to assure the victory.

Man had already been taken in 1313 and two years later Edward Bruce led his expedition to Ireland. A fair number of those who went with him were Highlanders and shared in both the initial apparent triumphs and the final, bitter, desperate and ultimately doomed *chevauchée* that brought Edward Bruce to his destiny at Faughart. Even if the intervention in Ireland proved futile, Clan Donald reaped other, highly tangible, rewards for their loyalty; all of the Macdougall lands in Lochaber, Ardnamurchan, Morvern and Glencoe came into their possession.

Bruce was generous but cautious; he was aware, like any previous incumbent of the Scottish throne, that too much power in the hands of a single family posed a latent threat of considerable magnitude. He was not seeking to promote another Somerled. Angus Og's loyalty was fashioned from his feud with the Macdougalls, certainly not from any innate patriotic fervour. The king must reward such sterling service; equally, he needed to build in the appropriate level of checks and balances.

Robert Stewart, the king's nephew and future sovereign, was given lands in Kintyre, thus extending the family's holdings in the west. While Angus Og did receive lands in Lochaber, this was largely a hollow gift, for the area was incorporated into Thomas Randolph's earldom of Moray. Neil Campbell of Lochawe, related to Bruce by marriage, scooped up territory in Argyll, the basis for the family's steady ascent thereafter. While so many garrison outposts had been deliberately slighted, Dunaverty was rebuilt as a royal hold, as was Tarbert. Dunstaffnage, the very centre of the Macdougall hegemony, was placed in the keeping of the Campbells.

Angus Og may have been dead by 1318; there is a suggestion that an Alexander of the Isles and one of the Macruaris fell with Edward Bruce in the course of his final defeat in Ireland. This Alexander appears to be the man earlier granted lands on Mull and Tiree, and there may have been some form of power struggle being played out in the west at this point. Angus Og had a natural son named John or Iain, known as *Iain Abrach* – John of Lochaber, from whose loins was sprung the smallest sept, Macdonald of Glencoe.[23]

'Good' John of Islay, who was to bring the lordship to its full maturity, came into his inheritance at a difficult moment in Scottish history when it seemed that all of King Robert's work might yet be undone and the spectre of English domination once again hung over the realm. The cause of these fresh disturbances was a class of landless magnates collectively referred to as the 'Disinherited'. The Treaty of Northampton was flawed, in that those nobles who had previously enjoyed the ownership of cross-border estate were excluded, without compensation, from their former lands in Scotland. Bruce was adamant, on his own behalf and that of his successors, that the Scottish polity should not be damaged by divided magnatial loyalties.

Certain men such as Umfraville, David of Strathbogie and Henry Beaumont were thus alienated from their expectations of lands north of the border. Beaumont had sought out Edward Balliol, the competent and warlike son of Toom Tabard, who had died quietly and virtually unnoticed, certainly unlamented, in comfortable exile. Edward III had made efforts through diplomatic channels to secure redress for the 'Disinherited', or at least some of them, but these negotiations achieved nothing. Bruce had already parcelled out the forfeited estates among his own followers.

Early in 1332, the 'Disinherited' were preparing to secure their right through force of arms and, while Edward would not openly permit any perceived breaches of the truce, he was happy to turn a blind eye as their small fleet assembled off Yorkshire. At the battle of Dupplin Moor, the invaders scored a signal triumph against superior forces commanded by the regent, the Earl of Mar, himself something of an Anglophile who may have been stung into launching a rash attack by allegations of treason hurled by Bruce's bastard son.

Both perished in the fight when English longbowmen, stationed on the flanks, shot such deadly volleys into the ranks of the schiltroms that the main and lesser flanking columns were herded into one great toiling mass, who were either spitted on the spears in the centre or assailed by arrows from both sides. The slaughter was prodigious.

For Edward Balliol, the fruits of victory included a short tenure as *de facto* king of Scotland while the boy king, Bruce's son David II, was eclipsed. The usurpers' grip was so shaky that even at the coronation feast the guests remained in full harness throughout, and by the end of the year Balliol was surprised, routed and sent fleeing, half-clothed, back into England.

Edward III was forced to concede that his puppet could only be sustained by a substantial English presence, and the following year the king laid siege to Berwick. A bumbling attempt by Douglas to relieve the leaguer resulted in an even worse defeat for the Scots at Halidon Hill, just north-west of the town. Balliol was to enjoy a further, equally fraught, tenure as monarch, propped up by English bills.

John of Islay, exhibiting that finely honed caution which would characterise his political career, maintained a careful neutrality, being actively courted by both the Bruce and the Balliol factions but committing to neither. After the disaster at Halidon, Thomas Randolph, Earl of Moray, the new regent, paid court to John at Tarbert but had less tangible rewards to offer than Balliol, who inclined to reckless generosity in an effort to buy Clan Donald's support. The Earl of Ross had fallen at Halidon, leaving his own his wide estates and the confiscated Stewart holdings. Accepting the inevitable, John bent his knee to the king of England at Perth in 1335.

By September of the following year, his submission had secured possession of Skye, Lewis, Kintyre and Knapdale, together with a new charter confirming the grant of all his existing lands. Though Macdonald was happy to lend nominal support to Edward Balliol when it brought such sweeping gains, he appears to have done little in return. The usurper was prepared, through desperation, to accept the fact of a Macdonald hegemony in the west, far exceeding Somerled's domain, as the price of keeping John from the Bruce camp. From the English perspective, the creation of a strong semi-independent lordship in the west established a potential ally against a resurgent Scottish Crown.

However, the defeat and death of John of Strathbogie at Culbean marked a further resurgence of the patriot cause, and Balliol's regime tottered. As John of Islay clearly discerned, the plain fact was that only English arms kept Balliol on his shaky throne; once the field army was withdrawn the whole crumbling edifice of Balliol kingship would collapse. By 1338 Edward III had dallied long enough in Scotland; he had a far bigger game to play. The death of the last of the Capetian kings of France ten years earlier and the rise of Valois created an opportunity for Edward, through his mother, to launch a bid. This was contemptuously rebuffed and at the time the king was in no position to back his claim with force. A decade on, matters had changed.

By this time John of Islay, for the first time, was styling himself in correspondence as *Dominus Insularum* ('Lord of the Isles'), a semi-regal title, recalling the earlier appellation of *Ri Innse Gall* ('King of the Hebrides').[24] As the Balliol cause faltered, John seamlessly transferred his attentions to the usurpers' patron Edward III, thus distancing himself from failure and treating with the king of England, himself also styled *Dominus Hibernie* ('Lord of Ireland'), almost on equal terms.

When the young king of Scots, David II, was able to return in 1341, the Bruce faction viewed John of the Isles as a potential enemy, and for a while he was declared traitor. In real terms, however, the Bruce affinity could no more afford to alienate Macdonald than the despised usurper. The price of compromise was the loss of Skye, which reverted to Ross, together with Kintyre and Knapdale, which were returned to Robert Stewart, the king's cousin and the future Robert II.

All in all, John had done quite well from the civil war, and at no cost in blood or treasure. He now proceeded to carry out another signal coup, marrying Amy Macruari, the only living relative of Ranald, who held the lordship of Gamoran comprising Knoydart, Moidart, Arisaig and Morar, together with the islands of Uist, Barra, Eigg and Rhum.

In 1346 preparations for a major foray into northern England were disrupted when Macruari, John's brother-in-law, was murdered near

Perth, allegedly in consequence of a dispute with William, Earl of Ross. If so, Ross gained nothing from his crime; John, on the other hand, came into the Macruari lands, in right of his wife, and he could not avoid the taint of complicity.

By this time England and France had been at war for a number of years. Edward III's early land campaigns had gobbled up vast resources for no tangible gains. In 1340 he had won a major naval engagement at Sluys, and an outbreak of civil strife in Brittany provided a foothold, with each monarch supporting opposing candidates for the dukedom. For his campaign in 1346 Edward landed in Normandy, and he finally brought the French to battle on the field of Crécy in August. Here the stout yeomen of England with their prodigious archery humbled the pride of French chivalry and asserted the supremacy of English arms.

In October David II, with a large force, crossed the border and ravaged Northumberland; he appeared before the walls of Durham and made camp in the Prince Bishop's hunting reserve of Beau Repaire (Bearpark). If he believed, as he appeared to, that he could equal his father's achievement in establishing total military supremacy over the shires of northern England, he was mistaken. Edward III was infinitely more competent than his hedonistic father and he had left the defence of the region in the capable hands of the northern magnates, who would not be cowed by the Scots.

A confused mêlée in thick mist, during which Douglas with the van was discomfited, heralded the unexpected presence of an English host on 17 October. King David, still refusing to believe the threat was potent, allowed the English to assume an ideal deployment on high ground just west of the city of Durham while his army, in three columns of schiltroms, lumbered forward with no proper reconnaissance. Douglas, leading the left-hand brigade, was soon in difficulties in the uneven terrain. The king in the centre and Stewart on the right achieved initial success, but their attack was held and the battle devolved into a grinding, hard-fought slog.

The Stewart withdrew his men, after they had been checked by Balliol, leading the English cavalry reserve, but while the issue still hung very much in the balance. His excessive caution or wilful defection left the centre horribly exposed and ultimately doomed. The Scots were badly mauled and the king, already wounded by arrows, was taken while hiding beneath the span of Aldin Grange Bridge. It was a disaster.[25]

With the king now a captive in England, John of the Isles was free to consolidate his earlier gains unfettered by royal interference. So confident was he of his power that he felt able to permit some remnants of the despised Macdougalls to resettle in Lorn. In one sense, he had brilliantly recreated Somerled's old kingdom, but the Lordship was much less of a Celtic institution. John exercised power as a great feudal magnate rather than as a Gaelic chieftain. His background was firmly rooted in the Celtic tradition, but his governance and practices were feudal. Tanistry, though still practised in Ireland,[26] no longer obtained in the Highlands. Primogeniture had become the norm; younger sons were still provided for, but by means of feudal grant rather than fee simple.

As a Gael, John held sway over his Islesmen, but he acted on the Scottish stage as a senior political figure in a feudal kingdom. He had proved adept at playing various factions off against the other; his triumphs were exercises in diplomacy rather than war. In practical terms, he had nothing in common with his freebooting Norse Gael ancestors. He eschewed the sword and achieved by the pen; when he made a grant of land it was by formal feudal charter, such as any of his magnatial contemporaries in both Scotland and England might have issued.

Donald, John's eldest son from his second marriage succeeded him, while Donald's brother, another John, remained a tanist during his lifetime. It was Donald's son Alexander who inherited on his father's death. In 1350 John pulled off another major coup, taking, as his second wife, Margaret, the daughter of Robert Stewart, heir apparent to the childless and still captive David II.[27] This was a very important alliance, drawing the Lordship into the Stewart affinity. Robert was regent during the king's captivity and relations between the two were always strained.

Thereafter John resisted, or at least did not respond to, overtures from Edward III, who remained happy to encourage any fissiparous tendencies that might weaken the northern kingdom. In spite of this, his relations with David II were never destined to be entirely cordial; his inclusion in the Stewart camp won no favours and the king refused to ratify his assumption of the Macruari lands. John was implicated in the Stewart rising of 1369 and showed no eagerness to submit following its failure. In spite of this, he lost nothing – the king might frown or fume but John was deeply entrenched. Nonetheless, Donald, the heir, another son and a grandson were temporarily held in Dumbarton Castle as pledges.

John fully came into his own when David II died suddenly, still without issue, in 1371 and Robert Stewart became King Robert II. The new king did not hesitate to confirm his brother-in-law's title to the Macruari lands, to which were added his current wife's inheritance in Kintyre. Astute as ever, John determined that he should be succeeded not by Ranald, the eldest son of his first marriage, but by Donald, born of his subsequent union with Margaret Stewart. Ranald was to be compensated by a grant of all of the Macruari lands his mother had brought, and his descendants thereafter formed the Clanranald sept.[28]

As a leading feudal lord, John, from time to time, occupied a number of important state appointments. He was constable of Edinburgh Castle and sometimes acted as proxy High Steward. He travelled to Flanders to negotiate the borrowing of portions of King David's ransom, a debt which placed a huge burden on the country's thin resources.[29] The rebellion of 1369 was partly a protest against the high levels of taxation needed to fund the periodic payments as they fell due.

The Lordship flourished through John's careful politics. While steadily increasing his power, he never overtly challenged the Scottish state; he flirted with England but never to the point of treason. He ruthlessly and ably exploited the contending factions for his own ends, promised much and did little. He never fought a battle but never tasted defeat. His cunning and circumspection were qualities his descendants would have done well to emulate. When he finally died in 1387 he had raised the Lordship to dizzy heights and his passing was marked with due solemnity and pomp, as *The Book of Clanranald* records:

> Having received the body of Christ and having been anointed, his fair body was brought to Icolumcille [Iona] and the abbot and the monks and the vicars came to meet him, as was the custom to meet the body of the kings of Fionnghall, and his service and waking were honourably performed during eight days and eight nights, and he was laid in the same grave as his father.[30]

Donald, the eldest son by Margaret Stewart, now assumed the Lordship unopposed and indeed supported by his older half-brother Ranald of Gamoran, who, again according to *The Book of Clanranald*, persuaded the seemingly reluctant chiefs to accept the much younger and untried son:

Ranald, the son of John, was High Steward over the Isles and the time of his father's death, being in advanced age and ruling over them. On the death of his father he called a meeting of the nobles of the Isles and of his bretheren at one place, and Donald was nominated Macdonald and Donald of Isla, contrary to the opinion of the men of the Isles.[31]

Donald also had two younger brothers. One of these, John, the Tanist, was granted lands around Dunyveg Castle. He married Marjory Bisset, in whose right he acquired title to the Glens of Antrim, and his Irish descendants formed Clan Iain Mor.[32] A second brother, Alasdair, took lands in Lochaber; his son, Alasdair Carrach, progenitor of Macdonald of Keppoch, fought both at Harlaw in 1411 and twenty years later at Inverlochy.

If Donald was a great feudal magnate, he was also the heir to a still-vibrant Celtic tradition. The later clan historian Hugh Macdonald[33] provides a glimpse of the ritual intensity of the ceremony attaching to his accession:

There was a square stone, seven or eight feet long, and the tract of a man's foot cut thereon, upon which he stood, denoting he should walk in the footsteps and uprightness of his predecessors, and that his was installed by right of his predecessors.[34]

Such a splendid pageant harks back to the early days of Dunadd and the ancient kingdom of Dalriada. Donald might rank as one of the greatest of the great feudal magnates but, unlike any of his peers, his was a Gaelic inheritance that was established long before feudalism supplanted Celtic practice. John of Islay, whom the Church had named 'the Good' on account of his many endowments, a practice his son continued,[35] had managed this dual identity with brilliance and élan and had profited thereby.

He had also benefited from the relative weakness of David II's position – a child king born into the savage uncertainty of civil war, continuing hostilities with England and the disastrous burden of the French alliance, subjected to long years of impotent captivity and unable to build a lasting affinity.

Donald inherited a stable and viable Lordship; through blood and marriage he was related to most of the Highland and Island clans – the Macleans, Mackinnons, Macduffies, Macquarries, the Macmillans and Mackays of Ugdale, the Maceacherns, Macnicols, Camerons, Mackintoshes, Macleods and Macneills. The Lordship had in its service dynasties of doctors (Beaton) and its own lawyers (Morrison).

While he had many residences, the two most important were Ardtornish in Morvern and the palatial complex constructed on two islets in Loch Finlaggan on Islay. Finlaggan was the administrative heart of the Lordship, not a fortress but a civil settlement mainly in timber, with a refinement of style that might be the envy of many contemporaries who still thought primarily of castle walls. It is a fitting comment on the stability that John of the Isles had created that he, the greatest of feudal magnates, did not require the security of a heavily fortified dwelling.

Stability did not, perhaps ironically, bring lasting security. While the Lordship was expanding, John and later Donald could acquire additional parcels of land with which to reward their hungry followers. If there were no continuing extensions, then there would be no new estates to grant which, of itself, would stimulate the emergence of fissiparous tendencies.

Donald took a clear pride in his Stewart blood; on his seal the traditional motif of the Hebridean galley is joined by the royal treasure of the Stewart kings. On a more practical level, the relationship between Donald, his brothers of the whole blood and their widowed mother quickly became acrimonious. A mere two years after John's death, his brother-in-law, John Stewart, Earl of Carrick, the eldest sibling and heir to Robert II, lodged a formal complaint against what he alleged was the mistreatment of his sister by her own sons. This family dispute dragged on into the next decade and reached such a pitch that in 1394 Carrick, now Robert III, instructed his brother Fife to take their sister under his protection.

A further, potentially explosive, cause of contention arose four years later in 1398, when Donald's youngest brother, Alexander, Lord of Lochaber, clashed with the Earl of Moray amid claims from the latter that Alexander was levying blackmail, or 'black rent' as it was then known.[36] The matter flared into violence when Alexander's caterans seized Castle Urquhart; it required a royal expedition led by the Dukes of Rothesay and Albany to restore order and to compel assurances from Donald and his brother. Outright hostilities were avoided, but relations were clearly strained and Donald failed to exhibit that acute sense of opportunism and deft political handling demonstrated so often by his father.

Alexander might have been checked but he was by no means chastened. Following the precedent set by his uncle, the Wolf of Badenoch, his caterans took up the burgh of Elgin in 1402. This time, however, the raiders spared the cathedral and its precincts. Three months after the outrage, Alexander and his followers did due penance, made adequate compensation including, from Alexander, a magnificent gold necklace or torque, and duly received absolution.[37]

Donald now had to face a serious internal threat. His other brother, John Mor Tanister, who remained next in line until Donald produced an heir and who had been granted lands on Islay and in Kintyre, now rebelled. Quite what sparked this internecine squabble is unclear, although contemporaries pointed the finger of blame at the Green Abbot of Finon, a member of Clan Mackinnon[38] who was described in a papal mandate as 'a dissolute who has squandered the goods of the monastery'.[39] His meddling proved abortive and John was obliged to flee, firstly to Galloway and then on to Ireland.

From Armagh, he offered his sword to Richard II of England (it was probably around now that he married Marjory Bisset). By 1401 he was being referred to as Lord of the Glens of Antrim in official correspondence, and by then appears to have been reconciled with his brother. His descendants by Marjory, the Macdonalds of Dunyveg and the Glen, were the forerunners of the Macdonnells of Antrim who emerged as a powerful sept on the later disintegration of the Lordship.[40]

Donald had experienced life at the English court in his boyhood, being sent there as a pledge for his father's ransom in 1369. The circumstances do not appear to have created a pejorative view and he, with his brothers, attended court on several occasions thereafter. He could expect to be treated as a distinguished guest with the status of a free prince; in 1400 he was furnished with an escort of eighty horse.[41]

By the turn of the fifteenth century, Donald seemed secure in his domain, but the cracks in his relationships with his Stewart kin were already showing. Both the king and Albany had taken their sister's part in the dispute which had arisen with her sons. The death of Rothesay and the disaster at Homildon propelled Albany back into the ascendancy, and his grip would hold fast until he finally died in 1420. Relations with his nephew Donald were destined to deteriorate dramatically.

4

The Earldom of Mar

Sen Alexander our king was deid,
That Scotland left in luf and le,
Away we sons of aill and breid,
Of wyne and walx, and gamin and gle.
The gold was changeit all in leid,
The frute failyet on euerilk tre.
Ihesu, succour and send remeid,
That stad is in perplexite.[1]

The medieval Scottish earldom of Mar was defined to the north and south by the floods of the Don and Dee respectively. The earldom of Angus lay southward over the high ground of the Mounth and the twin earldoms of Buchan and Moray stretched to the north-west. The earldom was a Celtic inheritance, descending through a line of Gaelic lords or *mormaers* until a break in the succession in the 1170s furnished William the Lion with the opportunity to grant his younger brother, David, the lordship of Garioch. His chief hold was the classic motte and bailey castle thrown up at the Bass of Inverurie.

David was not the only Anglo-Norman immigrant; a son of the Earl of Fife established a fief centred on Huntly Castle, while the Earls of Mar used Doune of Invernochty, some dozen miles upstream from the site of their future stronghold of Kildrummy. The fissiparous tendencies of the Gaelic survivors in Moray were firmly crushed in 1230 and from then on Mar became a strategically vital link between the centres of royal power in the south and the recently subjugated northern provinces.

Kildrummy was not constructed until well into the thirteenth century by William, the fifth earl, who held sway for nearly forty years, from c.1244–1281. This incumbent was a man of great power and influence at both local and national level. He held a succession of key Crown appointments, being heavily involved in the negotiations which resulted in the Treaty of Newcastle in 1244. He was created regent during the minority of Alexander III and, although he lost his position due to malign English meddling, he was resilient and accomplished enough to win it back!

From 1252–1255 and again from 1262–1277 he held the office of High Chamberlain. In between, he negotiated a mutual defence pact with Llewelyn of Wales, whereby neither Scotland nor the Welsh principalities would enter into a separate peace with England. Later, in 1264, he was one of the joint commissioners of the army which completed the annexation of the Hebrides after the repulse of the Norwegians at Largs.

The earl, despite the earlier antagonism in 1261, was one of those magnates to whom Henry III of England gave assurance over the wellbeing of the Scottish queen's unborn heir while she was on a state visit to her father's court. Nine years later, Earl William was appointed to lead a further embassy to England. No Earl of Mar before had exercised such influence on the national and indeed international stage; nor would any of his immediate successors, until the tenure of Alexander Stewart, achieve such prominence.

It was during the fifth earl's time that the province made the full and final transformation from a Celtic survival into a great feudal lordship and pillar of the emerging Scottish nation, a state founded on Anglo-Norman rather than Celtic practice. In the province itself, the great new feudal castle of Kildrummy was a potent statement in stone, a clear and constant reminder that there could be no return to the old ways.

Within the province, the earl, as befitted a great feudal magnate, enjoyed a very considerable degree of autonomy. He had his own household organised along semi-regal lines; he collected taxes and administered justice across the breadth of his estates; the lesser lords and gentry deferred to him and looked to him for advancement and patronage:

We must imagine the Earls of Mar in the thirteenth century as potent rulers, exercising an almost absolute sovereignty within their vast domains, and governing through their own officials and courts. It is difficult for us to conceive the enormous authority which in those early stages was vested in the great territorial magnates of Scotland. They had the power of pit and gallows over all their vassals; could call on them for military service, except insofar as touched their allegiance to the Crown; enjoyed all the multifarious dues in money, kind or service which characterised the feudal system of tenure; and appropriated all the fines inflicted in the baronial courts, not to speak of special revenues accruing from relief, ward, marriage, non entry, escheat and other casualties or occasional incomings. They were also the superiors of all burghs (other than royal or church burghs) or hamlets in the Earldom; and in return for the boon which their protection conferred on the inhabitants, took care freely to help themselves to the proceeds of their industry.[2]

The medieval Scottish Church had wide lands within the earldom, ruling these as would any lay magnate. Chief among the religious houses was the abbey of Lindores, founded some time before the end of the twelfth century. The earl represented the local pinnacle of the feudal pyramid; below him were the lesser lords and gentry, all owing military service, then free tenants, tenants at will, and beneath these the bondsmen and serfs. The lower levels were bound by labour rather than service; those at the very bottom tied or 'thirled' to the soil they tilled. Although unfree, they were not devoid of statutory protection, as the complex web of relationships between the grades of society in the feudal state were governed not only by custom but at law.

In 1296, however, the province of Mar experienced the first bitter taste of English warmongering. The hapless King John was forced by a noble junta into assuming an aggressive posture and fled to Strathcathro at the neck of the Cairnamounth Pass. He had no serious intention of offering further resistance and submitted on humiliating terms to Edward I on 7 July. Having dealt with his disobedient vassal, Longshanks crossed the Mounth by the Crynie Corse Pass and progressed in easy triumph through both Mar and Moray. On 14 July he received the submission of the burghesses of Aberdeen, who were joined by the gentry of the Garioch, the bishop and dean. The murderous sack of Berwick, an object lesson in frightfulness, had clearly shown the fate of those who dared to oppose the king's will.

By the end of the month he was holding court at Kildrummy, where those who had not previously made their submission hurried to do so. This was not yet an army of occupation; Edward was a feudal superior punishing a disobedient vassal and establishing order. Discipline within the English ranks appears to have been rigorously enforced.[3]

Longshanks might have thought the Scots had been thoroughly cowed and fully reminded of their feudal obligations, but in this he was seriously mistaken. The following year it was William Wallace who appeared, and in July he raided the garrison at Aberdeen. For a space of years, the north-east enjoyed relative immunity from the constant alarums elsewhere, but in the summer of 1303 Longshanks returned, again at the head of his army.

On 17 August Brechin Castle surrendered, though only after a stiff resistance. From 23–28 August the king remained at Aberdeen; by 4 September he had moved on to Banff and by 10 September he was at Elgin. The early autumn was spent at Kildrummy, where he supervised or instructed the commencement of further construction work which now began on the Snow Tower and north curtain wall.[4]

Earl Gratney, the seventh to bear the title, succeeded in 1297 and was dead by 1305, leaving a minor as heir. The new earl, Donald, was a nephew of Robert Bruce, who now acted as tutor or guardian. As part of the raft of administrative measures Longshanks put in place on 15 September 1305, Bruce's appointment as guardian of the young earl was confirmed, together with his custodianship of Kildrummy.

Bruce's murder of John Comyn and his own subsequent threadbare coronation ushered in a renewal of hostilities. On 26 June 1306, the Bruce faction was worsted in the fight at Methven by the English, under Aymer de Valence. The king of Scots, now a hunted outlaw, sent the queen (his second wife, Elizabeth de Burgh), his daughter by his first marriage, Marjory, his sister Mary and the Countess of Buchan to the relative safety of Kildrummy. The garrison was commanded by Sir Neil Bruce, the king's youngest brother, and by John of Strathbogie, Earl of Atholl:

> For thaim thocht thai mycht sekyrly
> Duell thar, quhill thai war victaillit weile,
> For swa stalwart wes the castell
> That it with strenth war hard to get
> Quhill that thar-in were men and mete.[5]

For all its great strength, the fortress proved to be more of a trap than a refuge. Longshanks was perfectly aware of its strategic importance. The

Prince of Wales, Edward of Caernarvon, supported by the seasoned Earls of Hereford and Gloucester, was despatched to command the leaguer. On 11 July the prince had received the surrender of Lochmaben, a vital hold in the Scottish West March, while the king advanced through Perth and Forteviot, across the Mounth to Kildrummy. The royal women were placed in sanctuary at Tain, possibly intending to flee to the remoteness of Orkney. However, they were taken captive by the Earl of Ross, who ruthlessly violated sanctuary to grab so valuable a prize.

Neil Bruce continued in brave if hopeless defiance. His few defenders beat off repeated assaults and held their position until a traitor within started a potentially disastrous fire, torching the irreplaceable grain stored in the 'mekill hall'. The survivors of the garrison surrendered on or before 13 September. As rebels they could expect no terms and Neil Bruce, *miles pulcherrimae juventus*, choked out his life at a rope's end in Berwick.

By the autumn of 1307 Bruce was strong enough to turn his vengeful attention on the Comyn heartlands of the north-east. In November the perfidious Ross hastened to submit and by the end of the year the king was in Mar. The bitter winter spent skulking in the hills around Drumblade took its toll on his health, which broke down badly. The ailing monarch was carried by litter to Strathbogie Castle and thence to Inverurie. Barely recovered, he summoned his iron will to lead his meagre forces in striking a decisive blow against the Comyns at Barra, lying between Inverurie and Old Meldrum, on Christmas Eve. The power of the Comyn faction in the region was irrevocably smashed:

> Thai chasyt thame with all that mayn,
> And sum thai tuk, and sum war slayn,
> The remanand war fleand ay;
> Quha had good hors got best away.[6]

Bruce followed up his victory with a savage wasting of his enemy's lands, the infamous 'herschip' of Buchan. The fight at Inverurie had not just marked the eclipse of the Comyns but also the swelling of the patriot cause, with the initiative now swinging, for the first time, in their favour. Bruce did not intend to relinquish the advantage so dearly won; when Aberdeen Castle surrendered it was slighted – that is to say, the defences were at least partially dismantled so it was no longer defensible. This policy was to be repeated with many of the strengths recovered by the patriots. Theirs was a guerrilla struggle of outpost and skirmish; it was prudent to deny the enemy the use of fixed defensible positions wherever possible.

Having secured Scotland's freedom in a major trial of arms at Bannockburn in 1314, Bruce was free to take the fight to the enemy – to wreak systematic havoc in northern England and extract from a cowed nobility and citizenry the funds to pay for the war's continuance, while at the same time mopping up the remaining garrisons. By the 1320s he was able to rule effectively and unopposed. A number of his affinity received lands in Mar. These included his loyal follower and armour-bearer William de Irvine, of Bonshaw in Bruce's lordship of Annandale, who on 1 February 1323 received a grant of the eastern part of the Forest of Drum and made his seat at Drum Castle. The remainder, known as the lands of Leys, went to Alexander Burnett of the Farningdoun, a Roxburgh laird.

Another who was set to rise was Sir Alexander Fraser, Bruce's brother-in-law. In 1325 he was granted the lordship of Cluny and in June of that year received, by royal charter, an estate in Cardney (now Cairnie in the parish of Skene). The citizens of Aberdeen had offered their king their support in the difficult years 1308–1309 and were not overlooked. Ten years on, in 1319, the burgesses received a charter for the royal forest of Stocket on the city's western fringe.

By the 1330s the grim spectre of civil strife, invasion and foreign dominance had returned. The disasters at Dupplin Moor and Halidon had heralded an era of violence and uncertainty, as Edward Balliol and the other 'Disinherited' clung to the gains they'd wrested from the patriots. By the autumn of 1335 matters were so serious that only a handful of fortresses were still held for the patriots, chief among these being Kildrummy. Here Christian Bruce, the late king's redoubtable sister, still flew the patriot banner. Before the walls was encamped David of Strathbogie, a chief among the 'Disinherited' who had seized the earldom of Atholl. His grudge was an ancient one; his wife was a daughter of the same Red Comyn whose blood Bruce had shed nearly thirty years before.

Strathbogie's leaguer was in breach of the subsisting truce but Kildrummy, the kernel of Bruce and patriot power in the north-east, was too tempting a prize to let slip. For the chatelaine, who had lost her first husband and three brothers in the earlier struggle, the situation was grim indeed. She was not one to give way to despair and the garrison, actively commanded by her captain, John Craig of Auchindoir, remained defiant. Christian's second husband, the regent, Sir Andrew Moray, begged leave from the English governor Sir William Montagu to raise the siege. Montagu was honourably bound to comply with Moray's request; the code of chivalry insisted a husband be permitted to march to the relief of his lady and, besides, if Moray were defeated the patriot cause would suffer a further, perhaps fatal, blow.

To raise the siege and confront Strathbogie, a formidable opponent, the regent could muster no more than 800 men.[7] He was seconded by Patrick Dunbar, Earl of March and Sir William Douglas, both experienced fighters. Moray's followers were few but Andrew Wyntoun judged them to be 'the floure of that half the Scottish se'.[8] Montagu, in observance of the truce, made no moves to reinforce Strathbogie and Moray marched northward. Pure chivalry was not the only consideration. The fall of Kildrummy would have been yet another setback for the patriot cause at a time when flagging morale urgently demanded a victory. Furthermore, Moray needed to bolster his own position, to demonstrate to his kindred and tenants that he was still their lord and capable of ejecting the attacker.

Appraised of his enemy's approach, Strathbogie reasoned that the siege could wait; if he could defeat Moray in the field then the castle's fall was pre-ordained. Marshalling his forces, which were certainly superior in numbers, he marched south through the Boultenstone Pass to take station north-east of Loch Davan. If he was going to seek a trial of arms, it behoved Strathbogie to strike fast and hard, before Moray could raise more men from his own lands around. This made sound tactical sense, but the earl was not able to prevent John Craig from drawing off a part of the garrison to support the relief force.

Strathbogie had chosen his ground with care, his forces deployed across an elevated position blocking the road to Kildrummy. If he persisted in his advance, Moray appeared to be in a position where he would be forced to attack uphill against superior odds, scarcely an enviable choice. Craig found the regent and his brigade at the Hall of Logie Ruthven, where he brought the welcome news that he knew of a path that, if successfully negotiated, would outflank the 'Disinherited' and place Moray in a position to deliver an attack from far more favourable ground.

Appropriately, it was on St Andrew's day (30 November) 1335 that the regent leading one column and Douglas the other completed a difficult night march of three long miles over particularly difficult terrain. Strathbogie was not taken completely by surprise and was able to dress the line to meet Douglas head-on. Cannily, Douglas drew up his own battalion on the south-facing slope above a ford over the Burn o' Vat below, a small stream that flows westward down the slope of Culbean Hill and into Loch Kinnord. Strathbogie rashly mistook this manoeuvre for faintheartedness and chose the moment to put in an attack.

Unlike his opponent, he had not paused to consider how an advance over the rough ground and past the swift-flowing stream would disorder his line. Douglas launched his own men in a sweeping downhill charge as the 'Disinherited' struggled over the cold waters of the burn, flushed with autumnal rains. At the same moment Moray, timing his move to perfection, appeared on the flanks. It was all over very quickly – Strathbogie, disdaining flight, died sword in hand; the rest of his army was markedly less enthusiastic:

> With that Schir Andro of Murraif [Murray]
> Come in on side sa sturdely
> With all thaim of his cumpany
> That in his cummyng, as thai say,
> He baire doune buskis in his way.[9]

Culbean was the boost the patriot cause so desperately needed; Kildrummy and the Bruce position in the north-east were saved, the Balliol faction greatly diminished. The patriot knight Alexander Gordon, who is credited with having dispatched his usurping predecessor with his own hand, succeeded to the earldom of Atholl.

There is some evidence to suggest that the province suffered as a result of the wars, though opportunities for piracy, looting and levying black rent abounded. In 1364 the bishop of Aberdeen appointed a single priest for the churches of Kildrummy and Clova, as their revenues had been so diminished and 'time and again devastated by war'.[10] Twenty-two years earlier Matthew Goblauch, the smith of Auld Bourtie, was forced to sell up, having been impoverished by the effects of constant strife.[11]

Despite these ravages, Mar offered further opportunities for land-hungry middle-ranking gentry. In the reign of David II, which was characterised by a period of uneasy calm when the king was taken by the English in the rout of Neville's Cross, more families either moved into the region or expanded on their existing holdings there. One of these was Sir Alexander Fraser of Cluny, who was granted a lease of Aboyne to swell the list of his estates. Later, a Fraser heiress married Sir William Keith, Marischal of Scotland and Laird of Hallforest.

At the same period the Forbes family, who originated in the middle Deeside area, were increasing their own holdings. They had estates between Kildrummy and Alford before 1271 and lost heavily for their defiance of Edward I in 1306. On 3 July 1364 King David ratified the grant from the Earl of Mar to John de Forbes of lands in Edinbanchory and Craiglogy in upper Glen Brux. These were strategically important 'frontier' fiefs covering the vital Rhynie Gap. John's son and successor, the first Lord Forbes, continued the family's rise.

Another newcomer was Sir Robert Erskine, the High Chamberlain of Scotland. In 1358 he received a grant of lands in the Garioch and Balhaggardy, Conglass, Inveramsay, Drumdurno and Pittodrie, from the Earl of Mar.[12] Sir Robert's son, Thomas, subsequently married Janet Keith, a great-granddaughter of Earl Gratney, and through this union the Erskines derived their claim to the earldom. The Leslies, a martial name, were constables of Inverurie under David II. Sir George, whose elder brother was the last to hold constabular office, is said to have been granted the fief of Balquhain in the early 1340s as a reward for his military service during the second phase of the Wars of Independence. The Leith family were minor gentry from Edingarioch who had interests in Aberdeen. William Leith of Barns and Ruthrieston, who was also provost of the city, cemented the family's rise when he wed a daughter (possibly illegitimate) of the eighth earl.[13]

In 1374 Thomas, Earl of Mar died without issue and his vast patrimony passed to his surviving sister and, by right of his wife, to her husband, the first Earl of Douglas. The Douglases were bred in war, their rise linked inextricably to the enmity with England. Sir James Douglas was one of Bruce's two great paladins and the first earl had, with the Earl of March, been instrumental in the revival of Scottish military fortunes. He and March had been steadily 'pinching out' the English salients or 'pales' in the marches and winning back fortresses and outposts. The second Earl Douglas, who also succeeded his father as Earl of Mar, carried the fight into England to die a heroic death on the moonlit field of Otterburn in August 1388.

Douglas left no male heir and Mar passed to his sister Isabella and to her husband, Sir Malcolm Drummond, 'a manful knycht bathe wise and

war'.[14] The new earl was King Robert II's brother-in-law and a sup-
porter of the ill-starred Duke of Rothesay; this inevitably made him an
enemy of Albany's.

As a token of his regard for his uncle and as tangible reward for his
support, Rothesay assigned to him his annuities from the customs dues
of Montrose and Aberdeen. This was a sizeable boost to the earl's already
considerable income. Even when Rothesay fell Sir Malcolm remained
loyal, a brave if injudicious stance, for very soon, like his patron, he:

…wes wyth slycht
Supprisit and takyn: baith day and nycht
Kepit in till strait tenouns…[15]

The earl lasted little longer in Albany's confinement than his nephew
had done; by November 1402 he was dead.

Having disposed of his nephew and his slight affinity, Albany was still
left with an unsatisfactory and potentially dangerous situation in the
north. The Earl of Ross died in 1402; Moray was among those captured
in the debacle at Homildon. Donald of the Isles, like his uncle Albany,
had aspirations in Ross; his brother Alexander, the Lord of Lochaber,
had ambitions in Moray – aims he was happy to pursue by force, raiding
Elgin on 3 July 1402.

This *chevauchée* was probably less destructive than that of Buchan
some dozen years earlier. Alexander and his caterans had avoided sacking
Church property but were, nonetheless, excommunicated by William
Spynie, bishop of Moray. Contrition followed, and by the first week
in October Alexander and his wild kerns were seeking forgiveness
and sworn to make due compensation.[16] This offered scant comfort to
Albany; Alexander still commanded a large company of caterans and the
Crown had little real power in the region.

The duke, therefore, could find no other recourse than to rehabilitate
his younger brother, the infamous Wolf, whom he had so successfully
marginalised previously. In 1402, the ageing royal brigand and his volatile sons returned to Crown service, and two years later we hear of
Buchan attending a session of the Exchequer in Perth to be reimbursed
his expenses, monies he had disbursed 'for the common good'.[17]

In that same month Hugh Fraser, Lord Lovat, assigned estates in the
county of Inverness to the Wolf for a consideration of £75 and the earl's

continued 'help and counsel'.[18] Fraser would otherwise have been of Moray's affinity, and the fact that he had transferred his allegiance or reached an understanding indicates that Buchan was creating his own following in Moray. His position was greatly consolidated by the grant of the royal castle of Inverness, which had been within Moray's sphere since the 1390s.

However, on 20 July 1405 the Wolf of Badenoch finally growled his last, and with him perished royal influence in the north. Albany had successfully recast his brother as a loyal adherent of the Crown, but Buchan's death now left a clear vacuum. As the Wolf's illness progressed in early July and it became obvious he would not recover, Albany immediately seems to have feared that his other nephew, Donald of the Isles, would descend upon Ross. The duke conferred with Robert III at Linlithgow on 2 July; by 11 July he had taken station at Dingwall, while the king followed. In the event, Albany's fears proved groundless and no clear threat emerged.

One of Buchan's sons, Alexander Stewart, having passed a wild youth as a 'leader of caterans', had consolidated his military reputation through distinguished service on the continent. Nineteenth-century writers blamed Alexander for the death of Sir Malcolm Drummond and asserted that he subsequently kidnapped the victim's widowed countess, Isabella, and forced her into a degrading marriage, by which nefarious means he became Earl of Mar.

However, this was not so. Albany was responsible for the earl's capture and subsequent death in prison. From November 1402 Albany's commissioners effectively controlled the affairs of the earldom, while the countess was no more than a hapless spectator. The Council of Mar was dominated by the Earl of Crawford and the Keiths, the Earl Marischal being Albany's father-in-law. The triumverate of Albany, Crawford and the Earl Marischal were promoting the succession of Sir Thomas Erskine or his son, Sir Robert, once the countess had followed her husband to the grave.[19]

These careful plans were suddenly upset in August 1404 when Albany, caught for once unawares, found his grip on Mar shattered by his own nephew, Alexander Stewart, who seized Kildrummy and the person of the countess in a *coup de main*. This was not, as nineteenth-century writers chose to conclude, a single act of opportunistic brigandage but a local reaction against the rule of Albany and his affinity. Many of the gentry, including the Irvines and their kindred, already at feud with the Keiths, resented the apparent rise of the Erskines and saw in Alexander a viable alternative.

Knowing that his uncle's impotence would be short-lived and the inevitable reaction swift, Alexander moved with commendable speed to consolidate his position. Whether the countess was a willing participant or merely resigned is unclear; she had no cause to love Albany, who had in all probability caused or connived at the murder of her husband and the seizure of her lands. The marriage contract entered into on 12 August transferred the entirety of her estate to her new and much younger husband.

The landless young knight now found himself in possession of the earldom of Mar, the lordship of the Garioch, the forest of Jedworth, and all of the countess's other lands and holdings plus a handsome annuity of 200 marks from the royal customs revenue. The agreement also went on to specify that this great inheritance should pass firstly to any children born of the union (given Countess Isabella's age, further children were unlikely) and failing any such issue to the heirs of Alexander Stewart.

The charter was witnessed by Alexander Waghorn (a member of Stewart's affinity) and a leavening of local gentry including Sir John Forbes, his son Alexander and kinsman Duncan, Alexander Irvine and several of the Aberdeen burghesses. This was not banditry but policy; these men were leading figures in Mar and the Garioch, united in opposition to the Albany/Erskine faction.

Dr Douglas Simpson falls in with the nineteenth-century view of Alexander Stewart as a ruthless robber baron who murdered his predecessor and 'got away' with his subsequent kidnapping of the widow through his proximity to the Duke of Albany. This is entirely incorrect, for the losers in these events were Albany himself and the aspiring Erskines.

The very last thing Alexander Stewart could expect was his uncle's seal of approval – quite the reverse. Albany would now seek to unseat him and overturn the marriage charter. Alexander was undoubtedly both opportunistic and ruthless, but his coup was facilitated and endorsed by the active support and participation of a sizeable proportion of the local gentry.

Albany had failed to appreciate the resentment bred by his seizure of Malcolm Drummond, a well-respected and popular earl, the continued resentment at the control of affairs exercised by his creatures Crawford and Keith, and his proposed imposition of a largely unknown family on the earldom. Alexander Stewart, as the son of the Wolf of Badenoch and a noted leader of caterans, could provide both good lordship and military security. He was a proven knight, despite the wild days of his youth, and clearly a man who could command respect and loyalty. The Lowland chronicler Bower commented on the change wrought in Alexander by the weight of his new responsibilities, all the more surprising in one who had been 'in his youth… very headstrong and wild and the… leader of a band of caterans. But later he came to his senses, and, being changed into another kind of man, ruled with acceptance nearly all of the country north of the Mounth.'[20]

Caught wrong-footed, Albany could rage at his nephew's temerity and the upset of his carefully laid plans but he was in no hurry to resolve the matter through a trial of arms. Alexander could draw on support from his brothers in Badenoch and could count on the backing of such powerful local figures as Forbes and Irvine. Albany's grip was shaken and the crisis even sparked a brief revival of the royal authority, so long quiescent. By the end of November the court was at Perth, where an acceptable compromise to resolve the impasse was sought. It is by no means improbable that Alexander would accept no other arbitrator than the king himself; he could scarcely expect impartiality from his other uncle!

Recovering from the unexpected reverse, Albany had assembled his own lobby from the earldom, including Crawford and Sir Robert Ogilvy of Carcary. This was the brother of Alexander Ogilvy of Auchterhouse, sheriff of Angus and a son of that Walter Ogilvy who, fighting alongside Crawford, had died in battle against Alexander's brothers at Glen Brerechan in 1392. He also held his lands in Carcary from John Erskine of Dun, Sir Robert's brother. It may be safely assumed that Ogilvy was no partisan of Alexander's.[21]

By 1 December Crawford and Ogilvy had arrived at Kildrummy to lay the court's proposals before the *de facto* earl and his new countess. That the talks proceeded amicably and productively is evidenced by the fact Isabella granted several parcels of land to Ogilvy – perhaps buying off his family's enmity, Alexander making atonement for the warrings of his brothers.[22]

The crucial distinction between the settlements of August and December 1404[23] was that under the terms of the latter Alexander was confirmed in all of his titles, but in life-rent only. Any children of the union with Isabella would inherit, but should she die childless then on Alexander's death the whole estate would pass to her nearest heirs – that is to say, to the Erskines. A very effective compromise arrangement that catered for the interests of both factions. Clearly this proved acceptable to Alexander.

Both sides had appreciated the need for compromise. Alexander could not ultimately continue in defiance of Albany and the Crown; equally, the duke saw the limitations on his ability to control events in the north-east and could not afford to permanently alienate his ambitious nephew.

Dr Douglas Simpson paints a vivid if disapproving picture of the investiture scene at Kildrummy:

> In the background the frowning Edwardian gatehouse, streaming with banners. Between its massive towers the deep-recessed portal, in front the drawbridge and the long trestled gangway spanning the wide, palisaded ditch. Beyond in the field is the little group of brilliant figures, principal witnesses of the strange transaction, with the countess herself in the middle; the grave faces of the ecclesiastics; the busy clerks and the lowering peasants and retainers, looking with scant favour upon the bold usurper. Dominating everything and everybody is the haughty figure of Sir Alexander Stewart himself, as, clad in shining mail, he crosses the bridge, superbly confident, and bends the knee in solemn mockery as he delivers over to his unhappy victim the keys of her castle. It is not improbable that Isabella, feeling her insecurity as a defenceless woman amid so many reckless chieftains, was motivated mainly by desire of a stalwart lord who, in return for the glittering prizes she could offer him, might be at least her protector in the troubles by which she was encompassed.[24]

On 15 and 21 January 1405, Robert III confirmed Alexander in virtually all of the territories his wife had transferred, with the exception of the barony of Cavers in Roxburghshire. Alexander Stewart was now securely Earl of Mar. Those who had supported him in his bold coup in August 1404 were given no grounds for regretting their decision. In the years following his elevation the new earl worked assiduously to provide good lordship and, in so doing, seems to have won over the many people who must have been uneasy with his former notoriety.

He succeeded where his father had failed. The Wolf was seen as a predator, not a protector; his son applied his military genius to generating feelings of security, rather than terror, among his tenants and neighbours. He was shrewd where his father had been domineering; in spite of the inauspicious beginning his relationship with his uncle Albany also matured into one of mutual respect and co-operation.

The duke was quick to appreciate his nephew's administrative and diplomatic talents and Mar grew rapidly into the role of leading magnate and even statesman. He was perceived as a bulwark of royal authority in the north-east and an effective counter to his cousin, Donald of the Isles, in the west: '...the ravening wolf replaced by the bristling but dependable guard dog'.[25]

Mar served with further distinction in Flanders and was rewarded with the lordship of Duffle in Brabant. He was later appointed High Admiral of Scotland and led a fleet in a raid on the coast of England. Thereafter, he acted as an ambassador in the truce negotiations of 1406. A renowned paladin of chivalry both in the field and the lists, Alexander Stewart had very definitely 'arrived'.

Nor did the earl neglect to foster good relations with the burghers of Aberdeen, the city of 'Bon Accord'. He appears to have developed a particular intimacy with Provost Davidson, a local entrepreneur who numbered a tavern in the Shiprow among his interests. The burgh records minute several payments for stirrup cups proffered to the earl. The two men also entered into a joint venture agreement as privateers, Davidson sourcing the ships and Mar finding the men at arms.

In 1410, one of their ships took a valuable cog out of Danzig en route to Flanders. The privateer's prize crew docked at Harfleur, where the port authorities impounded the vessel. The Scots cannily produced letters of safe conduct which the *Parlement* in Paris preferred to the claims of the rightful owners. Mar wrote a blandly dismissive letter to the no doubt outraged Senate of Danzig suggesting that it had been Dutch fishermen who had pirated their vessel![26]

The Danzig men were not convinced and a private naval war ensued. The Aberdeen men, however, appear to have had the upper hand; on 6 July 1412 a Hanseatic cog, bound for Scotland out of Rostock and loaded with salt flour and beer, was taken off Cape Lindesnaes. The pirates threatened to throw the unfortunate skipper, a Klaus Belleken, overboard. This was probably bluster, for the majority of the crew were set adrift in the boats, but some were carried captive to Aberdeen and put to work as forced labour on the earl's building programmes.[27]

In addition to castle building and privateering, the Earl of Mar also concerned himself with horse breeding, making an attempt to improve the native breeds (referred to by one writer as 'small, ambling nags, mostly geldings, uncurried, uncombed, unbridled')[28] by the importation of Hungarian stallions. By the end of 1410, however, it was obvious that serious storm clouds were brewing in the west and that the continued security of the north-east would rest almost entirely upon the able shoulders of Alexander Stewart, Earl of Mar.

5

Clash of Spears

O Children of Conn of the Hundred battles
now is the time for you to win recognition,
O raging whelps,
O sturdy bears,
O most sprightly lions,
O battle-loving warriors,
O brave heroic firebrands,
the children of Conn of the Hundred Battles,
O children of Conn remember
Hardihood in time of battle.

Brosnachadh catha[1]

To the Norse Gael, fighting was a way of life, the path of the warrior; heroic deeds in battle were the very stuff of a man's lasting fame and his combats were lauded by the bards in the halls of his chieftain and the bothies of his kin. His principal tactic was the offensive, a wild rush into the fray often 'against all reason, all odds'.[2] This kind of Homeric culture would reward the hero with status and renown; there was little room for other standards of excellence. Battle was an individual experience, the medium whereby the clansman proved himself in single combat or a succession of combats against worthy opponents. A glorious death was often to be embraced with equanimity – winning the fight was not necessarily all.

The charge, properly delivered, was a terrifying phenomenon and might often overcome superior forces by sheer élan. If it was checked, then the attack would stall and very likely fail. Large-scale pitched battles were, as in most areas of medieval warfare, relatively rare; Highland feuds most often manifested themselves in ambush and foray.[3]

Where the foe consisted of untrained Lowland levies, the sheer ferocity of the charge could easily vanquish an enemy who lacked the discipline or motivation to stand. The armies of the Gael were small, highly mobile columns of trained, individualistic fighters, united by a common purpose, an established leader and the powerful pull of kinship.

Ideally suited for irregular warfare fought out in the difficult and trackless terrain of the west, Highlanders tended to fare badly against organised armies, such as those fielded initially by Rome and then by the Anglo-Saxon kingdoms which followed. They had no response to a military system that could deliver onto the field large bodies of trained troops, well armed, well led and supported by the appropriate logistical train. In 1164, in the course of his final fight at Renfrew, Somerled's Norse Gaels proved to be no match for mounted knights and men at arms, who were unimpressed by both their numbers and élan.

From the thirteenth century onward the Isles were exporting fighting men to Ireland, where they formed famed mercenary families of *galloglaich* or 'gallowglass'.[4] Within Scotland, the clans supplied Lowland lairds with companies of caterans (*ceatharn*). As early as the 1340s, Robert the Steward, later Robert II, was employing caterans to uphold his control of Atholl and Badenoch.[5] As discussed in chapter 2, this reliance on mercenaries proved a major bone of contention with the established Anglo-Norman lay and ecclesiastical landlords in these provinces. Often unchecked, the cateran forces were accused of illegal squatting and exploitation of others lands, levying blackmail, engaging in forays and generally fomenting lawlessness.

To the Lowland landlord, cateran and Highlander became synonymous with brigandry, and this perception fuelled the growth of the cultural divide between Anglo-Norman and Norse Gael. Increasingly, the great clan magnates of the central and western Highlands came to rely on the employment of these household warriors for their military muscle. A similar system was developing in Ireland, where the elite class of gallowglass was supplemented by the hiring of professional men at arms or 'kernes'.[6]

In 1389 a dispute arose between John Dunbar, the Earl of Moray and the bishop of Moray. The earl, upon his oath or avower, denied liability for damage caused by caterans in his employ to sundry tenants of the diocese. The loss suffered by the bishop was tangible and, despite a lack of overt complicity, the earl was vicariously liable for the deeds of his retainers, who had failed in any way to indemnify the bishop. Having been obliged to pay appropriate compensation, the earl sought redress from the individuals described as evildoers or malefactors (*malefactoribus*) – an expression that was, in Lowland eyes, to become virtually synonymous with cateran.[7]

Some years later, John Dunbar's successor, Thomas, and the bishop of Moray both entered into an agreement or indenture with Alexander of the Isles whereby the latter, with his cateran forces, was to be retained for a term of seven years to defend the lands of both from incursion. This smacks of what in a later age might be described as 'protection' money; the consideration was a fixed fee of eighty marks.[8] The contract defined caterans as forces who moved between different areas, consuming the produce of each. This undoubtedly refers to a system of compulsory billeting, similar to the arrangement known as *buannacht*[9] which frequently obtained in Ireland during the same period. The billeting of troops on the civilian population by magnates who could not otherwise afford to house their men has never been popular and billeting would continue to arouse strident protests for several centuries to come.

By the end of the fourteenth century, the power of the Lordship of the Isles itself was largely reliant on the employment of substantial cateran forces. These had to be sufficient to overawe the lesser magnates and impose a level of order in a society frequently riven by internecine feuding. John of the Isles was described by one contemporary chronicler as having in his service 'a strong party of standing forces, under the command of Hector More Macillechoan, for defending Lochaber and the frontiers of the country from robbery and incursions of the rest of the Scots'.[10] In a sense, the spread of the Highland mercenary, either in the employ of his own chieftain or another lord, was both the cure and the ill. Only the use of caterans could guarantee order where disorder arose through the unlicensed activities of others of the same mould.

The depredations of caterans in his employ were a major cause of complaint against the Earl of Buchan, the Wolf of Badenoch, during the course of the General Council proceedings in the spring of 1385. The Wolf was censured for the depredations of his hirelings, seen to 'wander about, gather and shelter' within his lands and to harry both lay and ecclesiastical tenants without distinction or respite.[11] Nonetheless, his cateran forces acquitted themselves admirably in the field, when pitted against Lowland knights in the scrimmage at Glen Brerachan or Glascune.

Their Lowland contemporaries found these 'wild' Highlanders alien and uncouth; Fordun describes them as 'wild and untamed, rough and unbending… comely in form but unsightly in dress'. [12] John Major, writing in the sixteenth century, provides a more detailed and less partisan view:

> From the mid leg to the foot they go uncovered; their dress is, for an overgarment, a loose plaid and a shirt saffron dyed. They are armed with a bow and arrows, a broadsword and a small halbert. They always carry in their belt a strong dagger, single edged but of the sharpest. In time of war they cover the whole body with a coat of mail, made of iron rings, and in it they fight. The common folk among the Wild Scots go out to battle with the whole body clad in a linen garment sewed together in patchwork, well daubed with wax or with pitch, and with an overcoat of deerskin. [13]

The best contemporary evidence for the martial appearance of Highlanders in the late fourteenth and early fifteenth centuries is supplied by surviving grave slabs. The effigy of a Highland warrior at Killian shows that the main body defence consisted of a padded and quilted coat or aketon, which falls to the knees in a series of pronounced vertical pleats. It has full sleeves fashioned in the same manner, gathered or laced at the wrists, which would serve to deflect a thrust which would otherwise slide under the protection and disable the arm of the wearer. Some have additional protection on the vulnerable points, particularly the elbows, where a glancing cut could again maim or disable. The neck and shoulders, perhaps the most vulnerable areas of all, against which a downward swinging cut would be aimed, are covered with an aventail or pisane of fine mail. The head is protected by a conical helm or bascinet, open-faced, without visor or gorget. Some have additional plate defences to the calves called greaves, which provide security to the lower leg below the hem of the aketon.

In addition to the distinctive lobate pommelled swords, which will be considered below, most of the figures are depicted as carrying small shields of the 'shovel'-shaped pattern, little more than bucklers and probably intended more for punching and parrying than pure defence.

As Major describes, the aketon was sewn from linen and strengthened with a daubing of pitch. The combination of a relatively lightweight fabric body armour with mail additions provided a workable compromise between protection and mobility, the test of every armourer.

It was possible to encase a man in heavy plate so as to be almost invulnerable to the majority of blows, but this could only be achieved at a cost to mobility, which in terms of Highland warfare and terrain would have been entirely self-defeating. Likewise, most Lowland knights wore visors attached to their bascinets; this provided vital cover to the face, especially from arrows. The distinctive pointed visors, or 'pig faces', as they were known, provided excellent deflection but at a cost to all-round vision and also to airflow.

Those of higher status might have shirts of mail or haubergeons worn over the aketon. Mail is an excellent defence, relatively light, flexible and resilient. Without the padded aketon underneath, a crushing blow could still shatter bone and a powerful thrust could pierce the links. The padding worn underneath provided both significant extra protection and vital cushioning. In 1460 the writer Pitscottie described the Lord of the Isles's retainers as being 'all armed in Highland fashion with halbershownes [mail shirts]'.[14] An ordinance passed for the defence of the realm in the sixteenth century stipulated that Highlanders in Crown service were to wear 'habeorhonis' (mail haubergeons), 'steilbonnets' (helmets) and 'hektonis' (aketons).[15]

Grant refers to a prose poem in *The Book of Clanranald* which describes warriors in the service of John, the last true Lord of the Isles. Obviously this post dates the Harlaw period by six or seven decades and is subject to a degree of poetic embellishment, but it nonetheless conjures a vivid and romantic vision of the cateran arrayed for war in the service of his lord:

It was at that time came the warriors, the wise, glorious-fighting, close-worded, well-counselled, noble, highly noble, active of deeds, high spirited, gold armoured Fhionghall, namely, the badged, luckful, silk-standarded, active, fiercely-living Macleans; and the soldierly, spirited, brave Clan MacIan, together with the faithful, highly-hospitable tribes around their lord to instruct the powerful prince and counsel the hero, namely, the active champion of the Red Branch; and lively, vigorous troops with purple garments; and vast, loud-shouting, fierce, high-spirited parties; and beautifully coloured, bold, keenly encountering, stout-hearted, austere troops of a good army. And they were in well arranged battalions, namely, the proud, luminous-countenanced, finely-hued, bold, right-judging, goodly-gifting Clan Donald; the ready, prosperous, routing, very bold, right-judging Clanranald; the attacking, gold-shielded Clan Alister; the protecting, firm, hardy, well-enduring Macphees; the fierce, strong men, the Maclauchlans; the lively, vigorous, liberally-bestowing, courageous, austere, brown-shielded Macdougalls; the cheerful, chief-renowned, battle-harnessed Camerons; the inimical, passionate, hardy, Macniels; the manly, sanguinary, truly noble Mackinnons; the fierce, undaunted, great feated Macquarries; the brave, defending, foraging, valiant, heroic, ale-abounding Mackenzies; the active, spirited courteous, grant-bestowing Clan Morgan and the men of Sutherland came as a guard to the royal prince; and the powerful, lively, active, great-numbered, arrogant Mackintoshes, in a very large powerful force around the chief of Clan Chattan. There came along with these warriors, earls, princely high chiefs, knights, chiefs, lords, barons, and yeomen at one particular place, to the noble son of Alexander; and there numerous, rejoicing heroes, and powerful, active, fierce-sounding hosts gathered together.

This is the manner in which they appointed the powerful, fierce, active, mighty-deeded, white armoured, supreme King of the Gael, the terror-striking, leopard-like, awful, sanguinary, opposing, sharp-armed, fierce-attacking, ready-dexterous, powerful, steady, illustrious, full-subduing, furious, well-prepared, right-judging earl as he received on him the armour of conflict and strife against every tumult, that is, his fine tunic, beautifully embroidered, of fine-textured satin, ingeniously woven by ladies and their daughters; and that good tunic was put on him.

A silk jerkin, which was handsome, well-fitting, rich, highly-embroidered, beautiful, many coloured, artfully done, gusseted, corded, ornamented with the figures of foreign birds, with branches of burnished gold, a multiplicity of all kinds of embroidery on the sides of the costly jerkin. That jerkin was put on him to guard him against dangers.

A coat of mail, which was wide, well-meshed, light, of substantial steel, beautifully wrought, gold ornamented, with brilliant Danish gems. Such a mail-coat was possessed by the lithe Luga of Long Arms. John received a similar one in the name of the One Father to protect him in battles against the armies of his enemies. And there was put over that battle mail-coat an encircling belt, which was battle-victorious, brilliant with blue stones, powerful, showy, branchy, artificial, ridgy, hard with good clasps made of bronze, with figures of flying birds on its borders... and there was put over that an angular cape, gold-bordered, even, with blue stones, of fine material, pointed, precious, buckled, close fine, attractive, delectable, corded, ornamented, that the eye in continually looking at it would be melted by the brilliancy of the powerful cape.

[His sword] sharp, serviceable, long, very hard, sound, straight, of smooth surface, long-bladed and of equal power through its length. Mac-an-luin was the like of it, which Fionn the chief of the Feine had; or the sword of the victorious Osgar, in the celebrated battle of Ventry; or such another blade as Chuchhulain of the Red Branch had, the son of the peaceful Sualtam; or the fine, slaughtering sword of the battle-victorious Connal Cernach, by which was effected the Red Raid, and although celebrated were their names, John happened to have better than any of them.

And he put on his hands full military gloves that they should be a protection to the palms of his hands against the impression of the white ivory hilt made by the force of many blows in striking the powerful warriors.

[His axe] blue sided, thin, light, sharp-edged, substantial, of true steel re-melted.[16]

Away from the Highlands, the first attempt to impose a standard for equipping the fighting man according to his station had been made by Bruce's Parliament sitting at Scone in 1318. Any man who held lands worth £10 or more was obliged to furnish himself with sword, spear, plate or mail gauntlets, an aketon or haubergeon, bascinet or round iron pot helmet. Further down the social ladder, those owning chattels to the value of a cow must bear spear or bow.

These ordinances followed earlier attempts to standardise military equipment that had begun in England in the reign of Henry II. In 1181, his Assize of Arms listed the arms and armour to be borne by each according to his degree. The legislation was overhauled by Henry III in 1242 and revised by his son Edward I, 'Longshanks', some forty-odd years later. In 1295 the king, who would the following year invade Scotland to punish John Balliol, whom he perceived as nothing more than a rebellious vassal, issued further decrees. All who held lands worth

£40 or more must be prepared, on three weeks notice, to fight as paid retainers of the Crown. Each was to be armed and accoutred according to rank.

This was to all intents and purposes an early form of mass conscription, and a very unpopular one it was too. Undeterred, Edward made similar provision for the raising of an army for the Scots campaign.

The armies which followed his grandson, Edward III, into Scotland were both smaller and more professional in nature. The charge of cavalry, the great thunderous advance of the heavy horse, had given way to a refined tactical system that permitted missile troops, the archers, to work with dismounted men at arms and billmen. This was a battle-winning formula, tested at Dupplin Moor and refined at Halidon Hill. It would empower the English to win a series of stunning victories against the gallant but utterly unprepared chivalry of France in the opening phases of the Hundred Years War. Edward now relied on professional companies under experienced captains who contracted with the king on specified terms.

By the fourteenth century, armour was increasingly made up of purely plate defences, with the use of mail being limited to the areas where only a flexible defence would serve, such as the underarm or the groin. Plate was now worn at the back as well as the breast, throat and neck; two or more shaped gorget pieces were fitted over the mail facing or tippet of the bascinet. Helmets themselves were losing the distinctive angular lines of the early campaigns in the Hundred Years War and becoming more rounded and closer fitting; the distinctive pig face visors were also losing their sharp profile, again becoming more rounded. The lower rim of the visor now slipped under the protective edges of the gorget plates, which would serve to prevent an enemy achieving an ungentlemanly dagger thrust beneath the visor.

The breast plate was joined to the back by a hinged fastening on one side and then secured by straps on the other; more straps secured the plates at the shoulder. The armour defences for the upper thighs, called tassets, were held onto the body defences by straps and consisted of horizontal hoops. The necessary gap under the arms which was required to permit free movement of the arms could, as mentioned, be covered by sections of mail sewn to the canvas aketon or arming doublet worn beneath the harness, and also by small circular plates worn to the front and hung by a further strap from the shoulder plates.

1 A view of the motte at Inverurie. Traces such as these are perhaps the most concrete evidences of the spread of Norman influence under David I.

2 The present-day farm of Balhalgardy; the cairn said to mark the spot where Provost Davidson of Aberdeen fell lay just north-west of the farm buildings.

3 Looking south-east from present-day Harlaw toward the fields and the monument; the photograph is taken near to where the Liggar Stone may originally have stood – this prehistoric monolith was said to mark the spot where the corpses of female camp followers slain in the fight were interred.

4 The battlefield monument, designed by Dr William Kelly and financed by the City of Aberdeen to mark the 500th anniversary, but not formally unveiled until 1914, on the eve of a far more destructive conflict. The memorial is one of the largest and most commanding of its type in Britain; solid and austere in pink and grey granite, it attracted some unfavourable reviews at the time and is perhaps more noticeable than notable.

Above left: 5 The remains of Balquhain Castle; these date from the sixteenth century and no obviously discernible trace of the earlier fortification remains. The heroic and somewhat notorious castellan, Alexander Leslie, is said to have lost six of his sons on the field and to have erected one of the earliest memorials on the site to honour their sacrifice.

Above right: 6 Gilbert of Greenlaw; the grave slab now in Kinkell church. He wears a conical bascinet with breastplate under his tight fitting surcoat or 'coat armour'. His sword is typical of the distinctive Scottish pattern of the period.

Above: 7 The gatehouse of Kildrummy Castle, designed to protect the vulnerable entrance. This, despite its poor state of repair, is markedly similar in plan to that of Harlech and may well have been rebuilt by Edward I after the siege of 1306. If so, it is the only survival of Longshanks's building in Scotland.

Left: 8 and 9 Doune Castle. The impressive scale of the construction of this fourteenth-century castle was intended to reflect the prestige of the Duke of Albany and his eldest son Murdoch; much of the original work survives. In part the design owes something to the preceding century, but the great towers are square rather than circular.

10, 11 and 12 Castle Urquhart. Dramatically situated in the Great Glen, overlooking the dark and enigmatic waters of Loch Ness, this impressive fortress was the gateway to the western Highlands and was, from time to time, in the possession of the Lord of the Isles. The castle may already have existed in the reign of William the Lion and the natural rock formations lend themselves to the construction of motte and bailey.

Above: 13 Castle Tioram. A well-preserved west Highland castle at the base of the Ardnamurchan peninsula, similar to others such as Mingarry, perched on a rocky outcrop with an anchorage below the walls. This is not untypical of a chieftain's fortified residence of the late fourteenth or early fifteenth century. Following the final fall of the Lordship in 1493, the slide into the Age of Forays ensured that defence became a paramount concern.

Opposite above, left to right:
14 Fifteenth-century pavisse. The pavisse was a large wooden shield often used to provide protection in the field to a crossbowman while engaged in the cumbersome procedure of loading his weapon. It was normally carried slung on the back; often a second man would bear the shield.

15 and 16 Two fifteenth-century daggers. Daggers were everyday wear at all levels of society. In battle the dagger could be used to exploit weaknesses in an opponent's armour or to deliver the *coup de grâce* with a swift thrust through the visor, beneath the arms or into the genitals.

17 Fifteenth-century sword. In the fifteenth century, swords tended to develop longer and thinner blades of fine steel, intended primarily for thrusting. The section of the blade nearest the hilt ('ricasso') was often left blunt so the user could effect a double-handed grip for a determined thrust. Manuals such as Hans Talhoffer's *Manual of Swordfighting* were popular training guides.

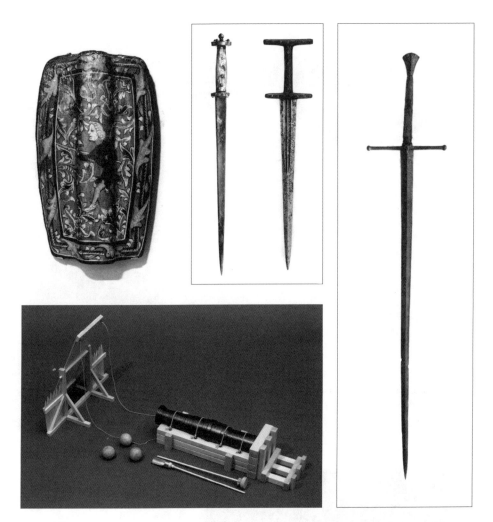

Above: 18 Model of a fifteenth-century bombard.
This shows the bombard in place for firing and the
gunners protected (to a degree) by a hinged wooden
shutter. The guns at this time were not mounted
on wheeled carriages; they were moved by cart and
then swung off to be laid in a firing position.

Right: 19 Bascinet, Italian, *c.*1390. The distinctive
'pig face' with its very pointed visor; the eye slots
and breathing holes are so fashioned that the point
of an enemy's weapon would be deflected from the
angled surface. The peak of the helm, raised from a
single section, is drawn to a point, also to facilitate
deflection.

20 Fifteenth-century knight's spur; a fine example of knightly accoutrement.

21 Mail shirt (haubergeon) and aventail, German, mid-fourteenth century. A longer garment made of fine mail. Constructed of a myriad of small, interlocking iron rings riveted together, the design had not altered significantly in centuries.

IACOBVS I D GRATIA REX SCOTORVM

22 Portrait of James I of Scotland. James spent most of his youth as a captive in England and did not return to Scotland until 1424. During this time his uncle, the Duke of Albany, ruled as regent and, as such, showed no particular enthusiasm for procuring the king's release.

23 Portrait of James II, who ascended the throne after his father was murdered in Perth. He bitterly resented the power of the Douglases and dedicated much of his kingship to breaking them; this included murdering the Earl of Douglas after supper at Stirling. Final victory over these overmighty subjects was achieved at Arkinholm in 1455. The young king was killed when one of his great guns burst on firing at the siege of Roxburgh in 1460.

Above left: 24 Portrait of James III, who like his father came to the throne as a minor. The least warlike of Scottish kings, he was more interested in literature, architecture and the arts. His coterie of base-born favourites and the taint of homosexuality exasperated the nobility, who took fearful revenge during the abortive campaign of 1482. James was later murdered; he 'fell into the hands of vile persons' in the aftermath of the rout at Sauchieburn in 1488.

Above right: 25 Portrait of James IV, Scotland's Renaissance prince, 'a glittering and tragic king' who ruled well and was responsible for many innovations. He is best remembered, however, for leading a Scottish national army to calamitous defeat at Flodden in 1513. It was he who finally abolished the Lordship of the Isles in 1493.

Left: 26 Halflang sword *c.*1450; long double-edged blade with deep fuller; elegant balance with a heavy, rounded pommel and distinctive downswept quillons.

Below left: 27 and 28 Longswords, possibly Scottish, 1400–1420. This is probably the type of 'long' sword referred to in the ballad, an elegant thrusting weapon with a distinctive lobate pommel, likely to have been carried by Lowlander and clansman alike at Harlaw and responsible for so much slaughter.

Right: 29 Grave slab of Reginaldus of Islay, who was the founder of Clan Ranald. Eldest living son of the Lord of the Isles by his marriage to Amy MacRuari, he died at Castle Tioram in 1386. He wears a conical bascinet, mail pisane and quilted aketon and carries a single-handed sword with straight quillons.

Above: 30 Highland clarsach, 'Queen Mary's Harp'. The clarsach was a small, portable harp, the universal accompaniment in the Highlands before the bagpipes. It provided an instrumental background to the essentially vocal lyric tradition.

Top right: 31 Seal of Robert II. Robert the Steward, first of the Stewart kings, when well into middle age came unexpectedly to the throne on the sudden death of David II in 1371. He oversaw a resurgence in Scottish fortunes after the resumption of hostilities with England in 1369, a careful blend of diplomacy and attrition.

Centre right: 32 Seal of Robert III , physically handicapped to an uncertain degree following an accident, and of melancholic temperament. Scotland was effectively ruled by the king's brother, the Duke of Albany, who wasted no opportunity to aggrandise his line, the Albany Stewarts.

Bottom right: 33 Seal of Murdoch, Duke of Albany.

The epic poem by Blind Harry, *The Wallace*, was written in the last quarter of the fifteenth century and when, in Book VIII, the author describes the hero arming for battle, the process he describes relates to his own time rather than to the thirteenth century:

> Quhen it was done Wallace can him aray
> In his armour, quhilk gudly was and gay
> His schenand schoys that burnyst was full beyn,
> His leg harnes, he clappyt on full fast,
> A clos byrny with mony sekyr cast
> Breyst plait, brasaris, that worthy was in wer.
>
> Besid him furth lop couth his basnet ber;
> His glytterand glowis grawin on athir sid.
> He semyt weill in battail till abid.
> His gud gyrdyll and syne his burly brand
> A staff off steyll he gryppyt in his hand.[17]

The majority of armours were imported from the great manufacturers in Milan, Germany and the Low Countries (a very fine Milanese foot armour from mid-century survives in the Kelvin Grove Museum in Glasgow). Notwithstanding this rush of imports, there were undoubtedly native armourers working in Scotland; most appear in the records of the sixteenth century, but a master named Moncur was active in Dundee in the 1440s.

Full harness was an expensive acquisition. In 1441 the English captain Sir John Cressy purchased an 'off the shelf' Milanese armour for £8 6s 8d; harness for a squire or man at arms of mass-produced munition quality might cost between £5 and £6.[18] For the discerning and wealthier client, bespoke armours would cost a great deal more. On the battlefield a knight might recognise armours worn by his comrades or his foes by their manufacture, an early example perhaps of the power of the 'brand'!

We have an excellent image of a knight from the day of Harlaw preserved on a grave slab in Kinkell churchyard, that of Sir Gilbert de Greenlau or Greenlaw, who may well have been a Lowland casualty. The figure is not complete – the lower third has gone – but we are left with the clearly incised representation of an armoured knight, and the carving, although by no means sophisticated, provides a first-class image of a man at arms from the exact period.

The inscription, which is regrettably incomplete, runs around the margin: 'Hic iacet noblis armiger Gilbertus de Grei... ANNO DMI. M. CCCC. XI'.[19] On either side of the knight's head is a 'heater'-shaped shield. The right side (dexter) is blank but the left (sinister) displays the paladin's arms; a chevron between two water budgets in chief and a hunting horn in base. The identical arms are depicted on the figure's outer fabric garment or coat armour. The water budget is the cognisance of the Greenlaw family and the knight was kin to the contemporary bishop of Aberdeen. The fact that the stone is dated to 1411 raises the possibility that Sir Gilbert fell in the fight.

As to his harness, the knight wears a conical bascinet which sweeps down at the sides to cover the ears and is fitted with two hinges for a detachable visor. The torso is protected by a haubergeon with plate defences over it and the close-fitting coat armour which had replaced the flowing surcoat of preceding centuries. His upper arms are protected by plate splints and fitted vambraces cover the lower arms. He wears mail leggings or chausses reinforced by steel splints. Around his hips is a broad and sturdy belt which supports a rondel dagger on one hip and his sword on the other. The latter conforms to the pattern of the period (see below).

His harness is not of the latest or perhaps even of the best type, but it may be taken to represent the armour of a Lowland laird of the period and would certainly afford him considerable protection, although in the final analysis this may be assumed to have been inadequate. The facial features are not distinguishable, but this is the nearest we are likely to come to gazing on the features of one who fought and most probably died in the battle.

The sword was essentially a gentleman's weapon and, as previously noted, a number are represented on Highland grave slabs of the period. The fourteenth-century effigy of Bricius Mackinnon from Iona shows a long broad-bladed broadsword with distinctive upward-pointing (i.e. toward the point) quillons, with lobe-shaped terminals. Projecting down either side of the blade from the hilt are metal sections called languets, which are intended to give the upper section of the blade additional protection. The pommel (that is, the section of steel which secures the top section of blade or tang through the hilt) was either segmented, wheel-shaped or, in later examples, globular, with the head of the tang projecting up through the top.

The example shown from the National Museum of Scotland (Illustration 28) has a wheel-shaped pommel with the quillons swelling slightly toward the tips and very short languets. The grip is less than four inches in length, quite small, indicating that though the weapon is long-bladed it was intended to be hefted in one hand. Other blades of the period were intended as hand and a half or 'halflang' swords that could be wielded in a double-handed grip.

An English commentator writing much later of the field of Pinkie in 1547 describes the Scots as hefting swords 'all notably brode and thin, of excedinge good temper and universally so made to slyce, so as I neuer sawe none so good, so think I it harde to deuyse ye better'.[20] Full double-handers, the famous Highland 'great' sword or *claidheamhmor*, do not appear until the sixteenth century and the image, however tempting, of caterans wielding these formidable blades at Harlaw would be a false one.

Most swords were manufactured in the workshops of Milan, Savoy and Cologne. These particularly Scottish types would have used imported blades, with the distinctive hilts being fashioned locally. A number of statutes of the era make provision for the importation of continental armours as part of general cargoes. Daggers were carried both as items of everyday dress and for use on the field. Rondel, quillon and 'ballock' knives[21] were all available. In battle these could be employed as a handy means of making certain of a fallen foe, with a swift and sure thrust through the eye slits in the visor.

The long-handled battle axe or gisarme, descended from the Danish axes of the Norsemen, was fully developed by the fifteenth century; not so the Highland Lochaber axe, which is not mentioned before 1501, when one was acquired by James IV. It is of course possible, indeed highly probable, that the Lochaber-type axe was in existence during the latter part of the fifteenth century, though it is unlikely that it was used at the time of Harlaw.

Major describes their use as slashing weapons by the 'Wild' Scots, though the appellation Lochaber may be derived from the fact that the area was well wooded and furnished the timber for the shafts of these weapons, which were common to the Highlands in general.[22] In its definitive form the Lochaber was a broad-headed axe blade, not unlike a halberd, mounted on an eight-foot pole, usually with a hook fitted to the top of the handle, very useful for dismounting cavalry opponents!

Full plate harness was well beyond the means of the bulk of the commons, the feudal levies who made up the majority of Lowland medieval armies. The humble spearman would be likely to rely for body protection on a padded jack or perhaps a brigandine. These were quilted garments of leather or canvas, sometimes stuffed with rags or tallow or, in the case of the more sophisticated brigandine, sewn with small metal plates between the layers of material so that only the riveted heads appeared through the outer fabric covering, providing a decorative effect. A couple of these plates, complete with the copper nails that fixed them together, have been found at Coldingham Priory near Berwick.

Some jacks had sleeves of mail, others only of fabric; it was commonplace to sew lengths of chain to the sleeves to give some protection against a downward cut. In 1481 a royal ordinance provided that those foot soldiers who did not possess leg harness were to wear jacks to the knee and those with armour could wear a shorter jack which would extend to below the hips and the top of the plate. On their heads, the foot would wear either a simple iron pot or 'knapscull' or, for the better equipped, the ubiquitous kettle hat of the period, which was fitted with a wide protective rim remarkably similar in appearance to the British infantryman's 'tin hat' of both world wars.[23]

Writing in a later period, the Italian diplomat and correspondent Dominic Mancini has left us a vivid portrait of a late-medieval army observed at first hand. The force he describes are the northern retainers of Richard, Duke of Gloucester, who had arrived in London in 1483 to lend their might to their lord's notorious usurpation of that year. He writes:

There is hardly any without a helmet, and none without bows and arrows; their bows and arrows are thicker and longer than those used by other nations, just as their bodies are stronger than other peoples for they seem to have hands and arms of iron. The range of their bows is no less than that of our arbalests; there hangs by the side of each a sword no less long than ours but heavy and thick as well. The sword is always accompanied by an iron shield [buckler]… they do not wear any metal armour on their breast or any other part of their body, except for the better sort who have breastplates and suits of armour. Indeed the common soldiery have more comfortable tunics that reach down below the loins and are stuffed with tow or some other soft material. They say the softer the tunics the better do they withstand the blows of arrows and swords, and besides that in summer they are lighter and in winter more serviceable than iron.[24]

The basic tactical formation of Lowland foot was the spear hedge, the schiltron or schiltrom. This was introduced by Wallace, prior to the battle of Falkirk, as a formation able to resist an attack by heavy horse. As such, it was successful, but proved desperately vulnerable to missile weapons; the redoubtable Welsh and English longbows decimated Wallace's spearmen. Bruce used the schiltrom in an offensive role to win his great victory at Bannockburn sixteen years later. Subsequent commanders were roundly defeated by a combination of dismounted men at arms, billmen and longbowmen, as at Dupplin Moor in 1332, Halidon Hill in 1333 and Homildon in 1402.

The spears themselves were traditionally 6 eln (18ft 6in) in length.[25] As the medieval period progressed, dwindling stocks of native timber fuelled the increasing need to import staves from Europe.[26] The schiltrom was not strictly a regular formation either in terms of numbers or deployment. The term derives from the old name for a shield wall – a linear defence – but the spear formations employed by medieval Scottish commanders tended to be more circular in shape. A round formation is equally strong at all points and cohesion is slightly easier to maintain. The schiltrom was probably initially deployed as a line, with the flanks being pulled progressively rearward until they met.

> Upon examination, the circular schlitrom proves to be a splendid formation for foot soldiers. It is easy to maintain, even on the move; it is difficult to breach; and it allows its commanders to remain very close to the action of the battle without unnecessary risk. It is formed by taking a line, and bending it until the flanks meet. The result is in theory a circle, but the resulting wall is more likely a rough oblong. Sergeants could keep the circle from shrinking as men were killed by filling the space with men from groups of reserves within the ring.[27]

The strength of the schiltrom may be likened to that of a great hedgehog – a bristling fury of steel-tipped spears that, so long as the outward pressure can be maintained throughout, is virtually unassailable by horse or foot. Sergeants and veterans within the concentric rings of staves would be able to work at maintaining cohesion and a steady outward pressure.

The schiltrom, if momentum could be maintained, was a formidable attacking formation, as Bruce demonstrated, but if obliged to cover any length of exposed terrain or broken or marshy ground it was extremely vulnerable to missiles. The English archers at Dupplin Moor, deployed on the flanks of the men at arms, loosed volley after volley into the smaller divisions flanking the main column. The men who survived were herded toward the rest, so the Scots became one great struggling mass, a perfect target for the archers who did fearful execution among them.

If, as at Falkirk, the stationary schiltroms were left unsupported by either their own missile troops or by cavalry, they would be relentlessly thinned by the bows until either sufficient gaps opened up to permit the horse to enter or the formation collapsed and the men sought refuge in flight. In either case, they stood to be ridden down and slaughtered by the horse.

For effective movement to be initiated and maintained, much depended on the sergeants being able to get the men moving and keep them advancing steadily in formation. In theory at least, all each man needed to do was to keep track of the man next to him. If the sergeants in the centre, facing the foe, drove the men forward by command and exhortation as well as by example and those on the flanks hurried their men to the fore, then the circle would deploy, as though from column into line. Not that these deployments would be particularly tidy, but maintaining outward pressure was the key to a successful advance.

On the field perfect cohesion would be well nigh impossible. The nature of the ground and the bodies of dead men and horses would all disrupt. Provided, however, the steady advance and continued outward pressure could be kept up, then the formation would remain potent. It was a giant steamroller, not unlike the classical Macedonian phalanx, that would crush and overwhelm the enemy line.

The individual captains would take position within the battalions; dismounted knights and men at arms would act as local commanders and 'stiffeners', providing additional leadership and rallying points. While the size of the unit was not fixed, the schiltrom would only function if the sergeants and officers could exercise effective control and the formation could move effectively over the ground. At Neville's Cross in 1346 the attacking Scots were deployed in three brigades moving probably in echelon. Each of these divisions contained three or four schiltroms which are thought to have numbered somewhere between 1,000–2,000 men apiece.[28]

When standing on the defensive, the leading rank would crouch with the butts of their spears firmly lodged in the turf, the points facing outward at about chest height. The second rank would level their staves from the shoulder and project forward, a wall of steel impenetrable as long as it held. Once the enemy's rush was checked, the front rank would recover their dressing and prepare to advance.

Scottish armies tended to be more generally threadbare than those of their southern neighbours. Nor did they require the vast logistical 'tail' that accompanied English invasions, as they were usually fighting on interior lines. Professor Barrow, citing the apparently well informed author of *The Life of Edward II*, records that the baggage train accompanying the king's vast feudal army, snaking its laborious way to disaster at Stirling in the hot early summer of 1314, could have stretched for twenty miles! Many chroniclers tended to the romantic when describing medieval armies on the move, waxing lyrical over the gorgeous silk trappings of knightly chargers, the fluttering pennons and proud banners displayed.

The reality was undoubtedly less colourful. Knights would not mount their precious destriers until contact was imminent, nor would they don their harness. The gentlemen would amble on palfreys, a gaggle of mounted retainers behind, while the commons trudged along in their dust. Medieval roads were at best deeply rutted tracks; rain and the passage of many feet turned them into quagmires. The foot would be unlikely to display any great enthusiasm, raised in the main by feudal levy, dragged from their fields and marshalled into shambling, ill co-ordinated columns – ragged, frequently barefoot, a riot of gear, ill-provisioned, untidy and unwilling.

The army was a sprawling host which required an array of trades to function: carpenters, wheelrights, farriers, smiths, armourers, bowyers, fletchers, surgeons, sutlers, wives and whores. Behind this were herds of cattle and flocks of sheep, driven by drovers and adding to the general noise, dust and filth. The very sight of these vast toiling columns filling the pastoral landscape would have terrorised local inhabitants, for whom the army's passage, be they foe or nominally friend, could only spell ruination.

We should not forget that medieval man, for the most part, lived in relative isolation in 'ferm toun', hamlet and steading. The spectacle of these armoured hordes crowding the valleys, scavenging the fields and pastures, filling the very skies with the vast din of their approach, would have represented a terror of biblical proportions. Terror would have been an entirely sensible response. Discipline was poor at best and often non-existent; the passage of armies was marked by plunder, rapine and extortion.

If the Norse Gael was motivated by his long martial tradition, the Lowland knight, as distinguished from the commons, belonged to the cult of chivalry. Much has been written about chivalry and it may be cynically observed that its moderating influences were frequently more noted in the breach than the observance. Nonetheless, chivalric principles would guide Scottish knights like the Earl of Mar and those gentlemen who followed him at Harlaw. The roots of the concept are buried in the Germanic tradition of an Anglo-Saxon past. By the early Middle Ages the cult of chivalry had been cannily endorsed by the Church, which blended Christian principle with martial honour.

The cult flourished in the thirteenth and fourteenth centuries when the knightly orders went forth to battle paynim hordes from the Middle East, through Spain to the Baltic. The profession of arms was the only career choice for a man of noble blood and his training began at an early age. We should quickly dispense with any images of armoured knights as clowns on horseback; theirs was a lifetime of training that produced levels of skill at arms, physical fitness and hardihood that would be the envy of the world's contemporary special forces.

Chroniclers of the fifteenth century frequently lament what they perceive as a decline in knightly virtues, but the author Jean le Beuil, writing mid-century in his treatise *Le Jouvencel*, offers us an insight into the mind of the chivalric knight:

What a joyous thing is war for many fine deeds are seen in its course, and many good lessons learnt from it... You love your comrade so much in war. When you see that your quarrel is just and your blood is fighting well, tears rise in your eyes. A great sweet feeling of loyalty and pity fills your heart on seeing your friend so valiantly exposing his body to execute and accomplish the command of our Creator. And you prepare to go and live or die with him, and for love not abandon him. And out of that there arises such a delectation, that he who has not tasted it is not fit to say what a delight is. Do you think that a man who does that fears death? Not at all; for he feels strengthened, he is so elated, that he does not know where he is. Truly he is afraid of nothing.[29]

Harlaw is perhaps an unusual campaign, in that there was never any doubt that the issue could only be settled by a trial of arms. Battle was by no means the common objective of all medieval commanders. Wars could be won without the hazard of a decisive encounter in the field. Laying waste the enemy's lands and destroying his fields and crops – frightfulness as an instrument of policy and military tactics – could be highly effective. This form of economic warfare had the dual effect of impoverishing the foe and significantly weakening the bond between lord and peasant. An essential element in the social contract that was feudalism consisted of the magnate's ability to protect his tenants. His prestige depended on it: what value a master who remains impotent while his enemies ravage at will?

On the continent, siege warfare dominated; the aggressive tactics of Edward III's contract armies, who actively sought battle, came as an unwelcome shock. In an earlier conflict in France, the Cathar or Albigensian Crusades[30] of the early thirteenth century, several decades of savage warfare saw only one major battle[31] but many prolonged and often desperate sieges.[32] During both principal phases of the Wars of Independence the Scots had made use of scorched earth to frustrate English invaders, cannily denying battle and allowing hunger to do the work. Of the many who fought at Harlaw, hardly any can have had prior experience of a major fight. Mar and some of his affinity had seen service in Flanders and many caterans would have drawn in anger, but there had not been a major battle in the north-east since Culbean, nearly eighty years before.

Medieval commanders were wary of battle, if for no other reason than that they lacked the means to control events once contact had taken place. Communications were basic; flags, trumpet calls and gallopers were employed to transmit commands on the field, but the reality was that once the battle was joined the commander would find it virtually impossible to direct events thereafter. Wallace's decision to fight at Falkirk had proved disastrous; Bruce understandably, agonised before committing his army on the second, decisive day of Bannockburn. David of Strathbogie's decision to accept the challenge at Culbean had led only to defeat and death.

Religion was a dominant influence in the lives of medieval men and women, perhaps never more so than on the field of battle. No army would advance to contact without first hearing mass and receiving absolution. The chronicler Froissart describes how two armies prepared for battle in 1339: 'the two armies got themselves in readiness, and heard mass, each lord among his own people and in his own quarters: many took the sacrament and confessed themselves'.[33]

Oratory also had its role. A commander's relationship with his host was more intimate than that in more recent armies; the forces involved were much smaller. He would know all of the gentry present – some, perhaps many, would be of his kin or wider affinity. Men followed their lords and through him their commander; he would share with them the hazard of the fight. No comfortable billet miles behind the line for him.

Bruce makes a powerful appeal to his assembled brigades, before leading them against the English arrayed below them on the Carse, in a speech recorded by Bernard, abbot of Arbroath:

> My lords, my people, accustomed to enjoy that full freedom for which in times gone by the Kings of Scotland have fought many a battle. For eight years or more I have struggled with much labour for my right to the Kingdom and for honourable liberty. I have lost brothers, friends and kinsmen. Your own kinsmen have been made captive, and bishops and priests are locked in prison. Our country's nobility has poured forth its blood in war. These barons you can see before you, clad in mail, are bent upon destroying me and obliterating my Kingdom, nay, our whole nation. They do not believe we can survive. They glory in their warhorses and equipment. For us, the name of the lord must be our hope of victory in battle… if you heartily repent of your sins you will be victorious, under God's command.[34]

Many battles of the period, particularly those fought between the English and French, began with a barrage of missiles, the arrow storm of legend. Harlaw was not to be such a battle. Both sides would have archers – the Highlanders and caterans favoured the bow – but there is no suggestion of an opening exchange. Mar advanced resolutely to the attack. Arrows aplenty would be shot by both sides, but missiles were not to determine either the course or outcome of the fight.

Arrows, nonetheless, would cause casualties on both sides. Death or wounding by arrow is more personal than from a modern, high-velocity bullet; there is none of the numbing shock of impact, and the agony of the wound is instant and palpable. While a well-harnessed man at arms enjoyed a fair degree of immunity, the same did not apply to the rank and file. The ordeal of archery would be intensely felt by untried men, drawn from the plough, who had never experienced anything similar – the insistent, hissing rain of death that transfixed comrades into writhing, shrieking bundles.

Once the two sides came to contact then the fight became extremely personal – the field obscured by great clouds of dust and steam; a man's vision heightened and yet blunted by the red mist of fear; the stink of sweat, urine, excrement and blood. Above all, the noise – the great, swelling, deafening crescendo of battle that exploded over the otherwise silent landscape, deadening the senses.

The combat was a sprawling, untidy mass of lunging spears and hacking blades. Men, half blind in harness, their vision further impaired by dust and racket, were soon assailed by raging thirst in the exhausting press of the mêlée. Few men died from a single stroke but a disabling wound, bringing the victim to the ground, would expose him to more and fatal blows, most likely a cut to the head or that decisive dagger thrust through the eyepiece into the brain – a horrible, agonising and by no means swift demise.

The rot, when it came, would start from the rear; the man engaged at the front would have no thought of flight, the white heat of battle guiding his strokes, but those behind, overcome by sudden terror, doubt or the panic of infected rumour, would be the first to flee, leaving the fighters dreadfully exposed and they themselves prey to an enemy who would have leisure to mount for the pursuit. Most casualties were sustained by the losing side in the course of the rout. Scattered individuals and groups who had lost all cohesion were prime targets for organised, mounted pursuers.

A graphic account of the likely fate of the vanquished is given by Abbot Whethamstede, writing of the rout of the Earl of Warwick's men at the second battle of St Albans in 1461, events to which the abbot may well have been an actual eyewitness:

> The southern men who were fiercer at the beginning, were broken quickly afterwards, and the more quickly because, looking back, they saw no one coming up from the main body of the King's army, or preparing to bring them help, whereupon they turned their backs on the northern men and fled. And the northern men seeing this pursued them

very swiftly on horseback; and catching a good many of them, ran them through with their lances.[35]

From the preceding century, a work entitled *The Vows of the Heron* describes how the man at arms's bravado diminishes the nearer he comes to actual contact:

> When we are in taverns, drinking strong wines, at our side the ladies we desire, looking on, with their smooth throats… their grey eyes shining back with smiling beauty nature calls on us to have desiring hearts, to struggle awaiting [their] thanks at the end. That we would conquer… Oliver and Roland. But when we are in the field, on our galloping chargers our shields round our necks and lances lowered… and our enemies are approaching us then we would rather be deep in some cavern.[36]

And what of the dead, those anonymous piles of mangled bodies, severed heads and hacked-off limbs the medieval illustrators so frequently portray? Fallen noblemen and gentry would be borne from the field by their surviving followers for suitable interment, but the mass of the commons were stripped and tumbled into grave pits dug on or adjacent to the field. One such mass burial was excavated in 1939–1940 at Visby in Sweden and more recently, in 1996, a grave pit from the battle of Towton, 'Palmsunday Field', of 1461, was discovered.

Towton was a particularly bloody fight, arguably the biggest and most sanguinary fought on British soil. The pit was found to contain the remains of thirty-seven individuals, twenty-nine of which formed complete skeletons. The bodies had not been thrown in at random but laid systematically and packed tightly to maximise space; Towton was a field where the grave diggers would have been exceptionally busy. The first to be interred were placed with their heads facing west, as befitted Christian burial, but others were laid over in the reverse orientation, expediency triumphing over religious observance. On forensic examination of the remains, it was discovered that the majority, in cases where the cause of death could be identified, had suffered traumatic head injuries. One had a very clearly defined square hole to the right-hand side of the skull which neatly fitted the profile of the top spike of a poleaxe, a very popular gentlemanly weapon of the period. Another had repeated slashing injuries to the side of the head, most likely caused by a series of downward sword cuts.[37]

All of the dead were males[38] between the ages of seventeen and fifty; four were under twenty and seven aged between twenty and twenty-five. Another eleven were between twenty-six and thirty-five, and eleven more were over thirty-five. The tallest would have been around 6ft, the shortest 5ft 2in, and the average around 5ft 8in. All had been in apparently robust physical condition. Several showed evidences of multiple wounds; in the most extreme case, one man had sustained a dozen blows to the head. Some displayed signs of earlier, healed wounds, clearly showing that if this had been their last battle it was not necessarily their first.

Forensic sculptors from the University of Manchester rebuilt the features of one of the dead, the oldest, who from his heavy build was quite possibly an archer, and thus gave us a glimpse of the face of a medieval soldier. This individual had, presumably in an earlier campaign, sustained a particularly severe facial wound probably caused by a swinging sword cut. The trauma would have been severe and yet the medieval surgeons had achieved a remarkable level of healing and reconstruction, though the sufferer was left with a massive lateral scar running down the left side of the face.

In this, he was almost certainly not unique. Most of those who fought would bear the scars. A European traveller, Gerhard von Wessel, witnessed the return of Edward IV's army into London from their victory at Barnet in 1471: '...many of their followers were wounded, mostly in the face or the lower part of the body, a very pitiable sight'.[39] And these men were the victors.

6

The Fiery Cross

Thair enemys to tak or slay,
Be dent of forss to gar them yield,
Quha war richt blyth to wise away,
And sae for feirdness tent the feild.

Battle of Harlaw

The earldom of Ross consisted of a great swathe of territory that stretched clear across the northern Highlands, and its wide-flung lands encompassed the Isle of Skye and most of what is now Ross and Cromarty. Its southern flank rested on Loch Ness. The earl owned detached parcels of land in Badenoch and the better part of the modern county of Nairn.

On 8 May 1402, Alexander Leslie, the Earl of Ross, died in his castle at Dingwall. His heir was his daughter Euphemia, a young girl, delicate in health and possibly handicapped. Next to her in line was her late father's sister, Lady Margaret Leslie, who was married to Donald of the Isles. The earl's widow was Albany's daughter, making the heiress – the 'little crook backed girl' – his granddaughter.

The regent wasted no time in seeking to establish practical control over his dead son-in-law's vast estate. By 15 March 1403 he, together with his brother-in-law Alexander Keith of Grandon, had seized the Aberdeenshire barony of Kingedward,[1] a key holding in the pattern of lordships held by the comital family. Establishing control of the rest proved less easy. By the late summer of 1407 Albany was sufficiently secure to be issuing charters from Dingwall and styling himself 'Lord of the Ward of Ross', a title both pompous and provocative, which sounded grander than the reality behind it.

Donald of the Isles could only view these developments with growing alarm. Since 1342 the Stewart hegemony had increased with relentless avarice. Since acquiring the earldom of Atholl in that year, the royal family had added a further string of earldoms to its titles: Strathearn (1357), Menteith (1361), Caithness (1375), Buchan (1382), and now also Mar (1405), together with the old Macdouall lordship of Lorn in the 1390s. Albany's carefully nurtured alliances with Clan Campbell threatened the Lordship of the Isles from the south, while the prospect of his gaining Ross would see Clan Donald hemmed in by the Stewarts and their affinity. This was intolerable.

Albany had not finished, quite the reverse. His strategy was now to persuade the hapless heiress to take the veil and retire from worldly concerns. If she did so, she was in legal and property owning terms a non-person, and would no longer be the proprietor of her estates. The regent proposed she should resign the earldom to her uncle, Albany's son, the Earl of Buchan. In so doing, she would ensure that the creeping Stewart hegemony quite rightly feared by Donald would be complete. Besides, by right of his wife, the Lord of the Isles had a stronger claim in law than Buchan. For either candidate, such a claim would only arise from the date Euphemia actually entered a convent.[2]

Donald's position was further imperilled with the death of Robert III and the capture of the young King James I in 1406. With Albany secure and unchecked in the regency and clearly in no particular hurry to ransom the new sovereign, he was free to pursue his dynastic designs on Ross. Donald's position was by no means hopeless; he was the dominant local magnate, with a substantive following which neither the regent nor any of the other leading families could effectively challenge. What transpired, therefore, was some form of internal power struggle within the earldom – a 'cold' war, with contending factions picking over the carcass of the comital holdings.

Some time after 1405 Donald was able to gain control of the vital bastion of Dingwall, although he had relinquished this before 1411. Albany clung to some vestige of control throughout, though this clearly fluctuated and was, at best, limited to the comital centres of power. Castles that could be garrisoned by Albany's men, whose ability to control the lands around was neither fixed nor certain. The death of the earl left a clear power vacuum which neither Donald nor the regent could effectively fill. With the inevitable decline in comital authority, other factions arose. In central and western Ross the powerful and hostile kindreds of the Mackenzies, Mathesons and Rosses of Balnagowan squabbled for supremacy.

Albany was not only active in Ross; he had interests in Central Perthshire, particularly in the earldom of Atholl, which was granted to him in free regality[3] for the remainder of the king's life by September 1403. On or around 28 April 1404 the duke effectively secured the complete alienation of the Crown's reversionary interest, with the grant in fee simple of the earldom to Albany's other brother, and staunch ally, Walter of Caithness.

At a stroke he had again greatly extended the sway of his own affinity and, at the same time, had gained control of Dumbarton Castle; both of these considerable gains were at the expense of the royal Stewart patrimony. Despite this blaze of acquisitions, Albany could never feel entirely free from the latent threat posed by the power of his nephew, Donald of the Isles. The marriage alliance with his father, John, had not secured any lasting amity, especially as Donald had experienced such acrimonious relations with his mother, whose cause had been championed by her brothers.

By the summer of 1411 Donald's frustration was to erupt into violence. So far he had shown restraint, but he had little cause to expect any satisfaction from his uncle Albany, especially where the regent, justly notorious for his rapacity, was putting forward one of his own sons as a candidate for Ross. The Ballad describes how 'Grit Donald' now swore to take the earldom by force of arms 'or ells be graithed in his graif'.[4]

To pursue his aim, he prepared to summon a host sufficient to overawe anything the regent could muster; it may be supposed that his prime objective was to mount a great show of force that would, by its very potency, deter any opposition. There is no evidence to suggest Donald was actively seeking a trial of arms; neither he nor his father, John of the Isles, had previously sought confrontation on this scale.

The muster was fixed at Ardtornish Castle, one of his most favoured residences, and the force he intended to field would, by the standards of the day, be considerable:

Richt far and neir baith up and doun;
Throw mount and muir, frae toun to toun
Allangst the land of Ross he roars...
Battle of Harlaw

Donald picked some 6,000 of his caterans and vassals as his strike force[5]; so great was the initial muster that he sent a number home. Beneath his banner by the walls of Ardtornish were gathered not only the septs of Clan Donald but the Macintoshes, Macleans,[6] Macleods, Camerons and Clan Chattan.[7]

The muster would be facilitated by the ancient clarion of the 'fiery cross' – this traditionally comprised two burnt or burning timbers to which was affixed a strip of linen, symbolically stained with blood. This potent talisman was carried in relay by runners from district to district as a call to arms. It appears to have been both swift and effective. Many years later, when rallying his people against the Jacobites of 1745, Campbell of Breadalbane sent out the fiery cross, which travelled some thirty-two miles around Loch Tay in three hours![8]

The spread of the fiery cross was attended by solemn ritual born from deep and abiding superstition. If a runner met with an armed man, this was a portent of good fortune and success in the battle to come. When the clan was gathered and marching to the muster, any game or vermin that crossed the path of the column, be it stag, hare or fox, must be killed, else bad luck would attend. Should a bare-footed woman appear or stray before the company, she must be seized and blood drawn from her forehead with the prick of a dagger.

Donald's decision to force the issue was one he had clearly not arrived at lightly. Both he and his father, during the whole of the latter's long tenure, had avoided direct confrontation with the Crown or its representatives. The present difficulty lay, at least in part, in the fact that the young king was an impotent or near-impotent captive in England and Albany, for all his wiles, lacked the full authority of the Lord's Anointed.

Hugh Macdonald gives the impression, probably erroneously, that the regent dared Donald to enforce his claim by the sword: 'The Lord of the Isles told the governor he would either lose all he had or gain the earldom of Ross, to which he had such a good title. The duke replied, he wished Donald to be so forward as to stick to what he said'.[9] It is more probable that neither party sought a trial of arms. Donald would be wary of open defiance against the Crown, even the regent, but Albany's position, equally, was by no means so unassailable that he would seek conclusions with the Lord of the Isles. Both had sought to gain control of Ross through diplomacy and manoeuvre; neither had achieved any concrete results. The breakdown of comital authority within the earldom probably affected Donald more, as his dominions were both adjacent and exposed. To see control pass irrevocably and completely to the Albany Stewarts would be to see his own power and hegemony in the west severely challenged.

While at the height of his power, the Wolf of Badenoch had acted as a brake on Albany's ambitions in the north-east. The rapprochement between the two brothers and the Wolf's resurgence before his death in 1405 had removed that comfort. Alexander Stewart's seizure of Mar in 1404, overturning Albany's own *coup de main* of two years earlier, appeared to upset the balance of power once again, but the eventual settlement of 1404 and Mar's apparent loyalty since gave Donald little cause for comfort.

Until now Donald appears to have followed his father's prudent example and been careful to avoid any dangerous flirtation with England. Since the victory at Homildon in 1402, the southerners had regained the military initiative in the long decades of war. Hotspur's rebellion the following year had to a degree destabilised the border again, but with Douglas and now the young king as captives, Henry IV had little to fear from Albany, who had little to gain from igniting further hostilities.

In August 1406, Donald's nephew Hector Maclean (*Ektor Makgillane*) was given safe conduct to travel to the English court and speak with the captive James, held since March and living alongside Owen Glendower's son Griffith in the Tower.[10] Five years later, just prior to the launching of the Harlaw campaign, Donald's chaplain John Lyon also journeyed south for confidential talks with Henry IV.[11] The nature and content of these discussions is not recorded, but the very fact that they took place at all does raise the possibility that Donald had made overtures to James I about an alliance or understanding with Henry IV, aimed at unseating or at least weakening Albany.

Negotiations over the ransoms for the haul of noble Scottish prisoners taken at Homildon continued. Henry, a month after Maclean's visit to James in the Tower, appointed John Dougan, the bishop of Down and Janico Dartasso, the Admiral of Ireland to enter into separate talks with Donald and his brother John. In April 1407, Dartasso's commission was renewed; seconded now by Christopher Preston, he was empowered to treat with the Lord of the Isles 'at pleasure'.[12] By 1409, relations between Donald and the Admiral were sufficiently cordial to promote a double marriage alliance.[13]

The substance of this series of negotiations has never been revealed. It is possible, even likely, that the matter of the pretender known as the 'Mammet', who had begun his career in Donald's kitchens and who was a useful pawn to Albany, was discussed. Whether other, more general incitements to defy the regent were broached must remain a matter of speculation.

Anything which sowed discord within the Scottish polity would be of interest to Henry. By treating with Donald in the guise of a free prince, the king could foment serious mayhem at no personal cost. James had no cause whatsoever to love his uncle and could doubtless foresee the long years of his captivity stretching ahead until natural causes removed his uncle. It is tempting therefore to see an element of English meddling, supported by James I, as a factor, perhaps even the prime factor, behind Donald's decision. To make war on the regent with the king's blessing and encouragement was hardly treasonable.

This supposition, while tempting, is of course entirely conjectural, but it does offer an alternative to the prevailing Lowland view that the Harlaw campaign was nothing more than an opportunistic foray on the grand scale whose sole objective was plunder, rapine and spoil. Such an interpretation flies in the face of Donald's entire career to date and the whole cautious history of his father's tenure.

Having mustered the host in Morvern and appointed Hector Maclean, a formidable warrior, as his captain, Donald chose not to advance eastwards through Lochaber, as might be expected but progressed instead through Wester Ross, landing at Strome prior to a descent on Dingwall. Obviously securing his hold on the comital seat was a necessary element in his strategy. The Mackays turned out to oppose the Islesmen and contest both castle and town, but were swiftly brushed aside. At Beauly his further advance to Inverness was resisted by Lord Lovat and his Fraser kin. This check was also easily overcome and though the royal castle proved too strong to storm, the town and its ancient bridge over the Moray Firth were given to the flames.

The Wardlaw Manuscript records the Highlanders' 'taking up' of Inverness and laments the burning of the bridge:

> the famousest and finest off oak in Brittain, burns most of the town, becaus they would not rise and concurr with him. John Cuming, a gentleman burgher in the town, putting on his armour and headpiece and

two-handed sword, made such stout resistance at this nearest end of the
bridge against the M'donels that... if there were ten more like him in
Inverness neither bridg nor brugh had been burnt.[14]

The sack and torching of Inverness has been cited as proof that Donald
intended to carry fire and sword through the north-eastern Lowlands.
While reprehensible, the destruction at Inverness was understandable, in
that the burgh represented a symbol of royal, that is to say the regent's,
authority. Its destruction would be a very tangible reminder to waverers
or Albany partisans as to where the real power lay.

How much actual support Donald enjoyed in Ross cannot be ascer-
tained; clearly local magnate families such as the Mackays and Frasers
resented his occupation, which denigrated their own local standing.
Equally, it is certain Donald was not without allies, for he was able to
gather reinforcements which may have swelled his host to as many as
10,000 before resuming his advance through Moray and Banff.

The Lowland lairds and burghesses of Aberdeen were in no doubt
that Donald intended to treat their city in a similar fashion. However,
the exact nature of the Lord of the Isles's intentions at this point remains
unclear. It is likely that his advance did not represent as tangible a threat
to the city as the understandably nervous citizens believed. In all probability, Donald continued his advance to occupy those parcels of land
which formed part of the earldom, namely the sheriffdoms of Banff,
Aberdeen and Kincardine. This would be entirely consistent with his
objective of securing his wife's inheritance by force, but does not necessarily imply that he intended to destroy Aberdeen. Other than mere
plunder, there was no strategic aim to be achieved; indeed, he would
merely foster opprobrium throughout the lands he intended to rule.

Aberdeen at this time was the major east-coast port. In 1396 the population had stood at around 3,000, a fair size for the period, especially in
a kingdom which had few large urban centres. Although some 125 miles
north of Edinburgh, the city was very much a Lowland centre whose
attention was focused over the grey waters of the North Sea and the trading opportunities it offered. William the Lion granted the first charter in
1179 and there were originally two settlements. The first, 'Old Aberdeen',
which grew up around St Machar's Cathedral and the port, clustered on
St Katherine's Hill. The famous university did not yet exist in 1411.[15] The
city had suffered on numerous occasions during the Wars of Independence

and had last been thoroughly torched by Edward III in 1336. By the time of Harlaw, the defences had been allowed to deteriorate.

It came as no surprise either to the Earl of Mar or the rest of the north-eastern gentry that Donald chose to enforce his claim to Ross by military action. In the depths of the preceding winter, Mar had hosted a lavish Christmas feast at Kildrummy. The former landless leader of cater- ans could boast a guest list that included all of the leading figures in the region. In addition to his own brother, Sir James Stewart, he invited the bishop of Aberdeen, Gilbert de Greenlaw, who was also Lord Chancellor of the realm. Other senior clerics present included Henry de Lichtoun, the rector of Kinkell, who was in the course of a distinguished career to become bishop of firstly Moray and latterly Aberdeen. These princes of the Church were joined by a bevy of lairds and Robert Davison, the provost of Aberdeen and boon companion of the earl.

This distinguished gathering was assembled for a more serious purpose than merely partaking of the earl's groaning table. They met to discuss how they would meet the threat from the west, which all now perceived to be imminent. Nor does it appear that any doubted that Aberdeen would be the prime objective of the Islesmen. Mar was the obvious choice for commander in chief. He was the principal landowner, now established and well regarded by his neighbours, a proven knight of out- standing valour and the regent's nephew. His strategy was simple: when the Highlanders attacked they must be met in open field. He had no plans for negotiation or cowering behind Kildrummy's strong walls. The men of the Garioch and the citizenry of Aberdeen looked to him for aggressive leadership – they were not to be disappointed.

In the spring, we may imagine feverish activity in the Lowlands as the storm clouds gathered in the west. The lairds would assemble their kin- dreds and tenantry; the Aberdonians would be drilling in readiness; war gear would be repaired and burnished. Mar would call out his own cateran companies to stand ready. The main question was from which immediate direction the blow would fall. Mar was unable to order a full muster until he could be sure by which route the clansmen would invade. The lairds thus remained on their own estates, armed and vigilant. The Forbes family were charged with securing the strategic pass of the Rhymie Gap, the 'high road' to Donside. It was now just a matter of waiting and being ready.

Donald was almost certainly not anticipating any serious opposition. In this, his intelligence sources failed him lamentably. He did not expect the confrontation which was to occur at Harlaw. He judged that the size and mettle of his host would be sufficient deterrent. With the smoking ruin of Inverness now behind him, his reinforcements gathered, Donald marched south toward Aberdeen along the line of the main connecting road, the King's Highway. The host thus spread down through the Enzie, through Strathbogie and into the Garioch. According to the Lowland chroniclers, fire and waste marked their passing, though these claims may have been subsequently exaggerated.

Even without widespread destruction, the presence of so large and menacing an army would have struck terror into the local populace. Inured, at least in part, to the isolated depredations and petty larceny of cateran bands, this was something altogether new and infinitely more menacing. So large a host had not been seen since Calgacus had mustered the tribes to defy Rome. The Highlanders fought for loot and glory; an abundance of the former would suffice.

The degree of discipline Donald was able to enforce must have been questionable. This army would not proceed in regular columns, toiling along established highways, but in semi-independent bands, each under its own captain and several groups under the banner of an individual chief, moving cross country, swift and fleet – no great trundling mass of wagons and carts, nor ragtag of tradesmen and sutlers. These men kept in their pouches the food they needed and carried their weapons and supplies about them. They would take freely anything that they deemed necessary or that took their fancy, and it would be a brave or foolhardy man who sought to bar their passage:

> Without resistans, as be said,
> Throu all these parts he stoutly past,
> Quhair sum war wae, and sum war glaid
> But Garioch was all aghast.
> To hinder this prowd enterprise.
> *Battle of Harlaw*

For those who sought glory as well as loot, the opportunity was about to arise.

7

The Reid Harlaw

To hinder this prowd Enterprise,
The stout and michty Erle of MARR
With all his men in arms did ryse,
Even frae Curgarf to Craigyvar,
And down the side of Don richt far,
Angus and Mearns did all convene
To fecht, or DONALD cam sae nar
The Royal Bruch of Aberdene.

Battle of Harlaw

Like Aberdeen, Inverurie was, as it remains, a royal burgh and one which occupies a strategic location at the confluence of the Don and Urie. The ancient motte and bailey earthwork, the Bass of Inverurie, guards these vital river crossings. Although the old fort was probably very much decayed by the early fifteenth century, it made an obvious muster point. Mar, who had led his own tenantry and wild cateran bands from Kildrummy, was joined by Sir Alexander Ogilvy, the sheriff of Angus, with the gentry, their retainers and the feudal levy.

It is said that Sir Alexander Irvine, coming in haste from his seat at Drum Castle, paused on a hillside in Skene to look back upon his home, as though knowing this would be his final glance. He also gave hurried instructions as to the disposal of his estate and the plans for his son's forthcoming wedding.

Throughout the short summer night of 23 July the army was mustering in Inverurie. Mar did not intend to loiter but to seize the tactical initiative and attack the Islesmen who, as his scouts would have advised, were encamped on the plateau north of the town. The bulk of the earl's forces would be untried levied men with no experience of battle. He was intending to pit his slender forces against a foe not only much stronger in numbers but with an army comprised of hardy clansmen inured to war. It was a dangerous gamble, but to sit on the defensive was unthinkable; once Donald became fully aware that his passage was to be contested, he could prepare and deploy accordingly. An element of surprise was Mar's only ace.

The ground around the conical mound of the Bass would have been a scene of feverish activity during the short hours of darkness; from time to time fresh contingents were arriving from Donside, Deeside, the Garioch and the Mearns. Marshalling the host would have been a formidable task. Few of these men would have served together previously; the levies, untrained and largely unready, would have to be drilled into companies and battalions in readiness for the march at dawn.[1]

Donald of the Isles appears to have been unaware of all this activity a scant two miles from his position, a lamentable failure of intelligence. Even with such a formidable host beneath his banner, it was unwise simply to assume that none would dare bar his passage. Nonetheless, he had chosen his ground well. His encampment was situated astride the plateau centred around the 'ferm toun' of Harlaw. To the west, the land falls sharply to the marshy bottom of the Urie; the wet ground and the subsequent scramble was a wholly impractical approach. Similarly, on the eastern flank the ridge drops into the equally wet defile of the Lochter Burn. Here the wet marshland and dank pools were extensive, rendering any approach equally fraught.[2]

The plateau itself was a stretch of featureless moorland, barren, rocky and for the most part uncultivated. Some arable strips would have existed around Harlaw – 'the toun of fair Harlaw' – and Balhalgardy, which was about a mile further south toward Inverurie. Roughly equidistant, to the north, was the posting station of Legatesden, all three linked by the track of the King's Highway running from Inverness to Aberdeen. Donald's encampment would have sprawled across the bare ground – a vast, anarchic mass of men and lifted beasts, looted carts piled with plunder, women and camp followers. For the most part the Highlanders would be dismounted, though the chiefs and wealthier tenants or tacksmen would be mounted on sturdy garrons.

Before cockcrow on 24 July the march began; having heard Mass, the Lowlanders formed their companies and set off through the town. Did the townspeople come out to see the army pass by? For them, the outcome of the day was vitally important. If Mar was defeated, the town would suffer the full horror of sacking by wild men whose blood would still be hot from battle, scarcely a prospect to be relished. The battalions tramped over the timber bridge at Howford, which had stood on that spot since 1235. Unlike the line of the present B9001, the King's Highway ran more to the west and ascended the plateau directly toward Balhalgardy; beyond that was the bare ground of the Pley Fauld.

The Lowlanders would have been spared sight of their enemy until they had marched past Balhalgardy, but once on the plateau, the quickening light would have revealed the vast spread of the enemy's leaguer, now buzzing like a hive of angry bees as Donald and his captains realised their peril:

> Presumeand on thair strength and Pryde
> Without all feir or ony Aw,
> Richt bauldie Battil did abyde
> Hard by the Town of fair HARLAW.
> *Battle of Harlaw*

As they advanced to contact, Mar's columns would have deployed into line. The men were to fight in two schiltroms. The earl appears to have intended an attack in echelon, repeating Bruce's successful tactics at Bannockburn nearly a century before. The men of Angus and the Mearns made up the first division, the vanguard, under the able leadership of Sir James Scrymgeour. Scrymgeour was the Constable of Dundee and hereditary standard bearer of Scotland, from a family which had liberally poured out its blood in Bruce's War of Independence. He was seconded by Sir Alexander Ogilvy.

Mar, with the Earl Marischal (Keith) and the Earl of Erroll (Hay), led the main body beneath the banners of the Irvines, Setons, Leiths and Leslies:

> And thus the Martial Erle of MARR
> Marcht with his men in richt Array
> Befoir the Enemie was aware,
> His Banner bauldly did display.
> *Battle of Harlaw*

The Keiths and the Irvines had, until virtually the eve of battle, been at deadly feud. Sir Alexander Irvine had quarrelled with the Earl Marischal of Hallforest Castle. The cause of the dispute was recited by a later writer,

Sir Robert Gordon of Gordonstown, who compiled his account early in the seventeenth century: 'Marshall's people brunt on[e] of Drum's children amongst kale wort and Drum burnt ye hall forrest and wasted sundry of his lands in revenge of yt wrong'.[3]

Irvine, tiring of the feud, had recently made overtures to the Keiths for a cessation; part of the proposed truce provisions was that his son would marry Elizabeth Keith. The wedding contract is dated some three months after the battle[4] and Irvine's supposed injunctions to his followers on the morning serves to indicate that resolving the dispute was still uppermost in his mind. Sir Alexander, a noted paladin, was among Mar's boon companions and both had served together overseas. In 1410 the knight had received, from the earl, a grant of lands at Auchindoir, a former fief of John of the Craig.[5]

If Donald had been unaware of the muster, the appearance of the Lowland army to his front must have been a very rude awakening; although he enjoyed a comfortable superiority in numbers, many of his clansmen were dispersed in foraging and, no doubt, some private looting. His was a clan army; the men would muster quickly beneath the banners of their chief, rallying to the war slogan and each bearing the badge of his affinity, be it bog oak, myrtle or heather.

Presently, the Highland host was pouring out from the camp, a steel-tipped avalanche, sweeping over the moor to collide with Mar's van roughly halfway between Harlaw and Balhalgardy. The thunderous clash of arms was terrific, the fierce élan of the Islesmen driving their opponents back. So the ballad (as opposed to the narrative poem) relates:

> The Hielanmen, wi' their lang swords[6]
> They laid on us fu' sair,
> An they drave back our merry men,
> Three acres breadth an' mair.[7]

If the van was pushed back as far as the ballad suggests, and there is no reason to doubt the distance mentioned, then it is a tribute to the Lowland officers present that the schiltrom held. The men of Angus and the Mearns were repulsed but neither broken nor routed, and the line of spears held. The fact that they gave ground was inconsequential. Equally, the ballad testifies to the fury of the charge and the likely disparity of numbers.

The fighting was undoubtedly savage and gallant Scrymgeour fell in this initial clash; if the schiltrom eventually held their ground, the cost was high to both sides, the lightly armoured clansmen falling in droves beneath the Lowland spears. At least one company from the schiltrom, or perhaps more, lost their collective note and withdrew or fled in disorder to the relative sanctuary of a cattle fold by Balhalgardy. Hhere they apparently 'sat out' the remainder of the battle.[8] Hugh Macdonald describes this phase of the conflict, although it must be noted that his account is far from impartial:

> The Earls of Marr and Buchan ordered their men in a main battle, and two small fronts; the right front was commanded by Lords Marishall and Erroll; the left by Sir Alexander Ogilvie, Sheriff of Angus. They encountered one another; their left wing was forced by Maclean, and the party on Macdonald's right was forced to give way. There was a great fold for keeping cattle behind them, into which they went. The Earl of Marr was forced to give ground and that wing was quite defeated. Marr and Erroll posted to Aberdeen, the rest of Macdonald's men followed the chase.[9]

By now, with the Lowland van checked and rebuffed, the Islesmen had the opportunity to deploy. Their own van, taking the right, was led by Donald's nephew, Hector Maclean of Duart, 'Red Hector of the Battles', a famous swordsman and proven captain, standing at the head of his clan. Donald himself, as befitted the Lord of the Isles, commanded in the centre; with him stood the Islesmen and the Macleods with John of Harris and Roderick of Lewis.

The left was taken by Callum Beg Mackintosh, who accepted the lesser honour (the right being the greater) on the assurance that Donald would compensate him for his forbearance with a grant of lands in Glengarry. John Mor, the Lord of the Isles's middle brother, commanded the reserve which comprised the Mackenzies and Cameron of Lochiel. The youngest brother, Alasdair Carrick, was, much to his disgust, kept from the fight. The Lordship might survive the loss of two brothers but scarcely all three![10] Donald's dispositions are confirmed by Hugh Macdonald:

> Macdonald set his men in order of battle as follows. He commanded himself the main battle, where he kept most of the Islanders, and with the Macleods, John of Harris and Roderick of Lewis. He ordered the rest

to the wings, the right commanded by Hector Roy Maclean and the left by Callum Beg Mackintosh. John More, Donald's brother, was placed with a detachment of the lightest and nimblest men as a reserve, either to assist the wings or main battle as the occasion required. To him was joined Mackenzie and Donald Cameron of Lochiel.[11] Alasdair Carrick was young, and therefore was, much against his will, set apart, lest the whole of the brothers should be hazarded at once.[12]

Mar's attempt at a co-ordinated attack in echelon had stalled and he has been criticised for his failure to provide earlier support to the hard-pressed ranks of the van. If we support Hugh Macdonald's view, which is far from reliable, the earl had deployed his forces in three divisions, with the central, and presumably much stronger, column flanked by two lesser brigades. Mar's predecessor, as regent, had tried this tactic with disastrous consequences at Dupplin Moor. What appears certain is that the earl's deployment had not gone smoothly, with a gap opening between the van and main body, leaving the former exposed to the rush of the Macleans from that wing of the Highland army.

The fight now became general, with the clansmen launching a series of charges against the Lowland spears. The engagement had ceased to be a battle of manoeuvre and had become one of attrition. No particular evidence of generalship can be discerned on the part of either commander; this was now very much a soldier's battle, a vicious, exhausting, hacking, stamping, bloody slog.

A man in full or part harness can function in the front line for a very restricted period, perhaps fifteen or twenty minutes at best. It therefore follows that the fight was not continuous but that from time to time both sides fell back, as though by arrangement, to draw breath, take water and order their lines. Such a gentlemanly arrangement seems utterly alien to our contemporary understanding of war but the chronicle sources confirm that such lulls in the fighting did take place.[13]

Dr Douglas Simpson has attempted, most probably correctly, to explain an apparent anomaly in the ballad which asserts that at this stage Sir Alexander Forbes withdraws his company from the line so they may recuperate, while he sends to his castle at Drumminor for his haubergeon. This sounds most odd: would he not have donned his mail before deploying? The ballad then has Forbes's men launching themselves back into the fight at the critical moment. The chronicler Hector

Boece describes a second phase in the battle as Mar's outlying contingents begin to come up 'marching to the sound of the guns', and, with their fresh numbers, succeed in tipping the balance.

The Forbes tradition is that Sir Alexander rendered quite exceptional service on the day, to the extent that Mar thereafter 'entertained such an extraordinary esteem of him that he entered into a noble friendship, sympathy, affection and agreeableness of humour and disposition, together with their constant and inseparable society so strictly cementing it, that it continued indissoluble until the Earle's death'.[14]

A more likely explanation of the Forbes's role in the battle, as advanced by Dr Douglas Simpson, is that they comprised a commanded party stationed, prior to the battle, on their own lands at Drumminor, Edinbanchory, Logie and Brux. These estates were located at the southern end of the vital Rhynie-Kildrummy gap. Though Mar had previously been aware of the advance of the Islesmen through Strathbogie, he could not have been sure whether they would continue their descent through the Garioch or whether they would seek to penetrate the Rhynie gap and Glen of Brux. Until he was absolutely certain, it was essential not to leave the pass uncovered and Forbes would have been the natural, indeed only, choice to command here. Once the Highlanders committed themselves to pass through Inverurie, then it would be expedient and safe to order Forbes to join the main body.

Forbes would thus force-march his retainers toward the field by way of Clatt, Leslie and Chapel o' Garioch, the 'Mar Road'. This could account for their late arrival and possibly decisive intervention. Obviously the Forbes account may be biased and Boece does assert that the contingents which came up after battle had been joined were thrown piecemeal into the line and suffered heavy loss. It is, however, difficult to see how Mar could have dealt otherwise with these late arrivals. His line was clearly under enormous pressure; casualties had been sustained and it is reasonable to agree with Hugh Macdonald, at least in part, that a section of the right had given way and now hung back.

Reinforcements were vital, and the earl would not have had the leisure to order them fully into a fresh brigade. Peter Marren, in his reconstruction of the battle, places Forbes on the right of Mar's line. This must be correct, for even if we discount the more glowing testimonials contained in the Forbes account, Mar would have cause to thank Sir Alexander if his timely arrival succeeded in stemming the rot on that flank.

The line continued to hold but the fight was long and bloody:

With doubtsome victory they dealt
The bludy battel lasted lang;
Ilk man his neighbour's force there felt,
The weakest aft times gat the wrang;
There was nae mows there them amang
Naething was heard but heavy knocks:
That echo made a dulfeu sang
Thereto resounding frae the rocks.
Battle of Harlaw

Major, although writing much later, still gives a vivid account of the fighting which has the ring of eyewitness testimony. In his day, accounts from survivors would still be current:

The wild Scots rushed upon them [the Lowlanders] in their fury as wild boars will do; hardly would any weapon make stand against their axes handled as they knew how to handle them; all around them was a very shambles of dead men, and when, stung by wounds, they were yet unable by reason of the long staves of the enemy to come to close quarters, they threw off their plaids and, as their custom was, did not hesitate to offer their naked bellies to the point of a spear. Now in close contact with the foe, no thought is theirs but of glorious death that availed them only if they might at the same time compass his death too. Once entered the heat of the conflict, even as one sheep will follow another, so they, and hold cheap their lives. The whole plateau is red with blood; from the higher points to the lower blood flows in streams. In blood the heroes fought, yea knee deep.[15]

Major may have given way to poetic impulse, no doubt influenced by the balladry, but his words convey a stark image of the full horror of the battle as they day wore on, both sides locked together like punch-drunk fighters in a bloody embrace. After checking Mar's advance, Donald's men could not achieve further headway, but neither could the earl's schiltroms break the Islesmen or do more than hold off their repeated rushes.

Provost Davidson and the three dozen burghers of Aberdeen who accompanied him onto the field, 'those chosen to go forth against the cateran',[16] were in the thick of the fight. This seems a rather paltry contingent from a population of some three thousand souls, but each of the burghesses may have had his own 'tail' of servants, retainers or apprentices. Davidson himself – innkeeper, local politician and privateer – fell fighting bravely in the mêlée. Those two notable paladins Maclean and Irvine met in single combat; a long and sanguinary duel followed until both fighters expired of their wounds:[17]

> Gude Sir Alexander Irving,
> The much renownit Laird of Drum,
> Nane in his days was bettir sene,
> Quhen they war semblit all and sum;
> To praise him we should not be dumm,
> For valour, witt and worthyness,
> To end his days he ther did cum,
> Quhois ransom is remeidyless.
> *Battle of Harlaw*

Through the long, hot summer's afternoon the slaughter went on; men half blinded by sweat and dust struggled to hold the heavy spears aloft, as wave after wave of shrieking Islesmen smashed against the line like fierce breakers crashing on the rocky shore. Neither would give way, though the dead carpeted the plateau, the stink of death and ordure polluting the overheated air. Those in harness would be furnace-hot; without water at regular intervals, they would as quickly succumb to dehydration as to enemy blows.

For an armoured man particularly, his concept of the battle was limited to the enemy immediately in front and his comrades on either side. Harness, while giving considerable protection, did not make a man invulnerable to blows. The great slashing arc of a 'halflang' sword or Highland axe could inflict a massive crushing blow that, delivered with full force, could shatter bone even if the cut did not penetrate the plate. If he lost the use of his sword arm or could no longer heft his stave, a man was as good as dead. He could expect to succumb to a flurry of blows that brought him down and then, unless he could be dragged clear of the press, to be finished off by a dagger thrust to the face or genitals. The unarmoured foot and Islesmen were even more vulnerable.

John Keegan describes the likely scene at a subsequent battle a mere four years after Harlaw, the field of Agincourt, and he considers how the

English archers, breaking ranks, 'set about' the French knights. There is neither glory nor chivalry, just killing, brutal and crude. So it would have been on 24 July, when lightly armed Highlanders or caterans 'set about' Lowland gentlemen in full harness:

'Setting about them' probably meant two or three against one, so that while an archer swung or lunged at the man-at-arms' front another dodged his sword arm to land him a mallet blow on the back of the head or an axe stroke behind the knee. Either would have toppled him and, once sprawling, he would have been helpless; a thrust into his face, if he were wearing a bascinet, into the slits of the visor, if he were wearing a close helmet, or through the mail of his armpit or groin, would have killed him outright or left him to bleed to death. Each act of execution need only have taken a few seconds; time enough for a flurry of thrusts clumsily parried, a fall, two or three to kneel over another on the ground, a few butcher's blows, a cry 'in extremis'.[18]

Only the onset of evening and the utter exhaustion of both sides brought an end to the awful carnage. The Lowland line had held, though the cost had been high. Besides Scrymgeour, Irvine, and Provost Davidson, many others, including Mar's nephew Sir William Abernethy of Saltoun, had fallen; the earl himself was sorely wounded. Among the dead lay Sir Alexander Straiton, Sir Robert Maule, Sir Thomas Murray, Adam de Skene[19] and William de Tulideff,[20] with a roll call of lesser gentry and many of the commons. The city of Aberdeen would mourn not just the death of the gallant provost, who for all his more shady entrepreneurial dealing had fought long and well, but others of the thirty-six burgesses who had marched out to fight the cateran:

'Twas the same band, returning all,
The living and the dead, for there
The frequent corses to the wall
Their wounded comrades feebly bare;
And there, unvisored, pale and dead,
Stretched on his steed, where torches shed
A dim and fitful ray,
The provost came, and o'er him spread
The town's broad banner lay.[21]

Dr Douglas Simpson points out that the author, George Buchanan, writing in the sixteenth century, was of the view that more renowned gentlemen died on that day than in any battles with the English for a very long period before. Probably the butcher's bill among the gentry had not been so high since Halidon Hill – certainly fewer men of note fell at Neville's Cross.[22] The total casualties sustained by Mar's army are impossible to state with any accuracy, although a figure of 500 dead and wounded would probably not be far short. By medieval standards the battle was a long one; Agincourt was over in an hour and very few lasted all day – Hastings and Towton, like Harlaw, are exceptions.

> But Donald's men at last gaif back;
> For thay war all out of array,
> The Earl of Marris men throw them brak,
> Persewing shairply in thair way,
> Thair enemys to tak or slay,
> Be dent of forss to gar them yield,
> Quha war richt blyth to wise away,
> And sae for feirdness tent the feild.
> *Battle of Harlaw*

The poet waxes lyrical over Mar's success, but to the wounded earl with his battered and bloodied survivors who slept that night on the field[23] it would have been impossible to know if they had won or whether the Islesmen would be back in the morning. But at dawn on 25 July the Lowlanders awoke, stiff, aching and no doubt apprehensive, to find that their enemy had gone and the field was theirs. Now might they call it victory.

The Highland host had vanished back whence they had come; in addition to Red Hector Maclean, perhaps as many as a thousand had lost their lives or been wounded on the field. The threat to Aberdeen had gone; for the Lowlands the battle spelt deliverance. Dr Douglas Simpson quotes the observations of John Hill Burton in assessing the impact of the fight on the Scottish polity:

> It was a practice in Scotland to favour the heirs of those slain in the great
> national battles against England, by exempting them from the feudal taxes
> on the succession to their estates, including the rights enjoyed by the supe-
> rior during the minority of his vassal. The records of northern land rights

show that this was extended to the families bereaved at Harlaw, and that the battle was even in this formal way treated as a national deliverance.[24]

The Lord of the Isles may have left the field to Mar, but Clan Donald did not regard the battle as a defeat. The *Annals of Loch Ce* claim: 'A great victory for MacDomhnaill of Alba over the foreigners of Alba'.[25] Later, sixteenth-century Gaels such as Denis Campbell, who had no reason to love Macdonald, considered the battle to have been a victory for the Gael:[26] 'Donald was only ever routed by the lowland poets, often more colourful than accurate in their depictions of the battle'.[27] Or, as the Gaelic ballad affirms:

> On Monandy at mornin'
> The battle it began;
> On Saturday at gloamin'
> Ye'd scarce tell wha had wan.[28]

Peter Marren quotes the words of Professor Ranald Patterson, whose summing up of the result is both balanced and perceptive:

> The battle showed that the forces of the two sides were, for the time being, too finely balanced for the one to prevail against the other. But the battle also raised to a higher pitch the antagonism between lowlander and highlander. The time for tolerance or easy assimilation had disappeared, but the time for a wholesale attack upon Gaelic culture and upon the separatist political tendencies of Gaeldom had not yet arrived.[29]

Harlaw was thus not an end or, as Churchill said, the beginning of the end but, as the great man might have observed, it does mark the end of a beginning. From now on, even though the Lordship had another eighty-odd years to run, its very existence was clearly a continued challenge to the authority of the Scottish Crown. The battle highlighted and confirmed the growing prejudice felt by many Lowlanders against the Gael. The price of deliverance had been very high; scarcely a family in the north-east would not have cause to mourn. Sacrifice on that scale inevitably took on the aspect of a national rather than a purely local tragedy and the enemy this time was as clearly defined as the English before, defined by language, dress, custom and allegiance. It would not be entirely fanciful to hear the echo of Harlaw reverberate around the field of Culloden so many years later, when the final act in the tragedy of Saxon *v*. Gael reached its merciless dénouement.

It is perhaps appropriate to conclude with Major's judicious summation of the fight:

> In the year fourteen hundred and eleven was fought that battle far famed among the Scots of harlaw. Donald, Earl of the Isles, with a valiant following of Wild Scots ten thousand strong aimed at the spoiling of Aberdeen, a town of mark, and other places; and against him Alexander Stewart, Earl of Mar and Alexander Ogilvy, Sheriff of Angus, gathered their men and at Harlaw met Donald of the Isles. Hot and fierce was the fight; nor was a battle with a foreign foe, and with so large a force, ever waged that was more full of jeopardy than this; so that in our games, when we were at the Grammar School, we were wont to form ourselves into opposite sides, and say that we wanted to play at the battle of Harlaw. Though it be more generally said among the common people that the Wild Scots were defeated I find the very opposite of this in the chroniclers; only, the Earl of the Isles was forced to retreat; and he counted amongst his men more of slain than did the civilised Scots. Yet these men did not put Donald to open rout, though they fiercely strove.[30]

8

The Reckoning

It is no joy without Clan Donald; it is no strength to
Be without them; the best race in the round world,
To them belongs every goodly man.

The noblest race of all created, in whom dwelt prowess
And terribleness; a race to whom tyrants bowed,
In whom dealt wisdom and piety

A race kindly, mighty valorous; a race the hottest in
Time of battle; a race gentlest among ladies,
And mightiest in warfare.

A race whose assembly was most numerous, the best in
Honour and esteem; a race that makes no war on
The Church, a race whose fear it was to be dispraised...

For sorrow and for sadness I have forsaken wisdom and
Learning; on their account I have forsaken all things;
It is no joy without Clan Donald.

Ni H-eibhneas gan Chlainn Domhnaill ('It is no joy without Clan Donald')[1]

Harlaw may have been seen as a deliverance but it had been a very close-run thing indeed. Albany's confidence in his martial nephew had been fully vindicated, but at considerable cost. Clan Donald had been rebuffed and seen off but certainly not destroyed, nor necessarily even chastened. Donald might present the battle as a victory; while this was largely propagandist, it was certainly no rout. What was certain was that he could not now hope to claim the earldom of Ross by force; in this he had failed.

What is much harder to evaluate, and where the chronicles are of little assistance, is the impact of Harlaw on the relations or perceived relations between Highlands and Lowlands, between Saxon and Gael. Did the red mist of Harlaw mark a significant deepening of the rift that was probably apparent before, or was it just an isolated incident – a feudal squabble that ended in bloodshed?

In the short term, the regent was quick to capitalise on Mar's success. He raised sufficient forces to sweep north into Ross and recapture Dingwall. In the summer of the following year, he was preparing a major expedition against the Isles when Donald agreed to submit and made his peace with Albany at Lochgilphead. The terms of the cessation are unclear and were evidently not onerous – to the extent that the annalists of Clan Donald were able to persist in denying that any submission took place![2]

In 1415 Euphemia of Ross finally took the veil and surrendered her right to her grandfather, who promptly created his younger son John, Earl of Buchan as Earl of Ross. The reversionary rights were reserved to the Crown (as late as 1430 James I was claiming rights in Ross).[3] Buchan was not greatly interested in his role as Earl of Ross. The long war between England and France had flared again in 1415, when Henry V invaded Normandy and took Harfleur after a protracted and costly siege. At the close of the campaigning season he inflicted a crushing defeat on the French at Agincourt.

From then until his death seven years later, the king campaigned unceasingly to conquer Normandy and establish his right in France. He enjoyed many successes and while Albany ensured that Scotland, its young king still a captive, was not drawn into the renewal of hostilities, high-spirited knights like Buchan offered their swords to the beleaguered French. In 1421 Buchan led a Franco-Scottish force to victory at Beauge, where Henry's reckless brother Clarence was killed. The Scots involvement lasted until 1424, when the English regent, Bedford, decimated the Scots and their French allies at Verneuil; Buchan was among the slain.

In the Isles, Donald continued unchallenged; the reverse at Harlaw had not dented the Lordship's prestige. For the Gael, winning was not necessarily the prime objective – to fight well and perform valorous deeds was the true glory of war. Nor did Donald abandon his claims to Ross; in 1421 he is referred to in an entreaty to the Pope as 'Donald de Yle, Lord of the Isles and of the Earldom of Ross'.[4] In 1420 the octogenarian Albany finally died, his office of regent passing to his son Murdoch, who was but a pale shadow of his formidable father. James I at last returned to Scotland in 1424, by which time Donald too was dead, being succeeded by his son Alexander.

In terms of his relations with the Lordship, Murdoch, during his relatively short and undistinguished tenure, relied heavily on the agency of Colin Campbell of Lochawe. The Campbells, who had swelled to fill the void left by the Macdougalls, were proving useful servants of the Crown. Bound closely to the house of Stewart, they avoided the taint of Clan Donald's fissiparous tendencies and, although Gaels by birth and lineage, cannily became identified with the rising power of the Scottish Crown.

For James I, the end to his long captivity spelt the end of the Albany Stewarts. He was determined to destroy them. When Murdoch was imprisoned his son James rashly rose in rebellion, thus sealing his father's fate. James took and torched Dumbarton, killing the castellan, Sir John Stewart – the 'Red' Stewart of Dundonald, a bastard uncle of the king. When the rebellion failed, James fled to Ireland where he married into Clan Donald, forming an alliance with John Mor Tanister which most probably led to the subsequent murder of the latter.[5] James finally executed Murdoch, his father-in-law Lennox and two of his sons. As a result of these killings he recovered the three earldoms of Lennox, Fife and Menteith, while the power of the Albany Stewarts was utterly broken.

Hugh Macdonald sets the murder of John Mor Tanister against a sinister backdrop of royal jealousy. The king, swayed by the malicious entreaties of his court, sought to provoke Alexander into rebellion and proposed to use John Mor Tanister as his tool. According to Hugh Macdonald:

In the meantime the king sent John Campbell, to know if John More of Kintyre, Macdonald's uncle, would send to take all his nephew's lands; but it was a trap laid to weaken them that they might be the more easily conquered. James Campbell sent a man with a message to John of Kintyre, desiring him to meet him at a point called Ard du with some prudent gentlemen and that he had matters of consequence from the king to be imparted to him. John came to the place appointed with a small retinue, but James Campbell with a very great train, and told of the king's intentions of granting him all the lands possessed by Macdonald conditionally, if he would hold of him and serve him. John said he did not know wherein his nephew wronged the king and that his nephew was as deserving of his rights as he could be, and that he would not accept of those lands, nor serve for them... and that his nephew was as nearly related to the King as he could be. James Campbell, hearing the answer, said that he was the king's prisoner. John made all the resistance he could, till, overpowered by numbers, he was killed.[6]

At the outset, the Lord of the Isles had had every reason to celebrate the fall of the Albany Stewarts and thus enjoyed amiable relations with the king, but James, seeking to increase the royal authority, was not inclined to tolerate overmighty subjects in the west. As his principal agent, the king, like Albany before him, relied upon the Earl of Mar, but royal exasperation at what he perceived as the continued lawlessness of his Highland subjects continued to mount. As early as 1425 one of the king's enactments recognised the futility of bringing Highlanders within the bounds of law: 'The hieland men the quhilkis before the kingis hame cumyng commonly reft and slew ilk ane utheris'.[7]

In 1428 James's anger boiled over when he summoned some fifty chiefs,[8] including Alexander of the Isles and his mother, the Countess of Ross, to a Parliament at Inverness. There is in fact no evidence that any business of state was conducted; the summonses were a ruse to bring the chiefs within the king's power. Quite simply, it was a trap: the king summoned the Highlanders individually, 'warily and singly to his castle';[9] there they were seized and thrown into prison. The haul netted, in addition to Alexander and his mother, Angus Dhu Mackay and his four sons, Kenneth More Mackenzie, John Ross, William Lesly and Angus of Moray, the chief of the Mackmahons, together with Alexander Macruari of Gamoran and John Macarthur.[10] The last two were both executed; the rest escaped with greater leniency.

James felt this was a job well done. Major records how the king demonstrated:

> ...in the presence of his friends the pleasure that he felt in this occurence... [and] bent his face somewhat toward the ground, and then repeated before them these two verses which he himself had made, and here they are:

'Let us carry that gang to a fortress strong
For by Christ's own lot they did deadly wrong.'[11]

As a sop to the appearance of impartial justice, the alleged murderer of
John Mor Tanister, James Campbell, was also executed. This was mostly
to do with appeasing the great anger the killing had caused and, as Hugh
Macdonald relates:

> Campbell protested he had the King's authority for so doing, yet the king
> denied having given any other orders than that of apprehending him if he
> would not come into the terms proposed to him, and because Campbell
> had no written order from the king to produce to his defence, he was
> taken and beheaded, which shows the dangerous consequences of under-
> taking such a service without due circumspection.[12]

If this rough justice was an attempt to win 'hearts and minds', then it was
an inauspicious beginning. James's heavy-handed and duplicitous methods were not likely to impress. Alexander was, by comparison, treated
with understanding. His role in previous disturbances was attributed to
the folly of impetuous youth and the pernicious influence of bad advisors. After a short incarceration he was brought to court as a kind of
tame bear. If James thought becoming an unwilling courtier would 'civi-
lise' the Lord of the Isles and lead him to the wisdom of submission, he
was very much mistaken. The jealousy and taunts of the court alienated
him as effectively as imprisonment and he soon fled back to the west to
raise the standard of rebellion.[13]

The formal reconciliation between the king and Alexander of the Isles
had taken place on 28 August, a feast day, when the king, together with his
English queen, was attending Mass in the abbey of Holyrood. As the royal
couple knelt at the high altar Alexander entered the church, barefoot and
clad only in a light tunic, but bearing a drawn sword. This he presented
to James, symbolising that his life and lands were in the king's gift. At this
point the queen, fulfilling her womanly role, interceded on Alexander's
behalf and the king graciously assented. This had nothing whatsoever to
do with the queen's humanity but was a necessary element in the theatre
being enacted – to demonstrate the royal prerogative of mercy.[14]

This charade failed in its purpose. Like his father in 1411, Alexander
vented his wrath upon Inverness, the symbol of royal authority in the

north which was, neither for the first nor last time, given to the flames. In the rising the Lord of the Isles was steadfastly supported by Donald Balloch, Lord of Dunyveg and the Glens, son of the murdered John Mor Tanister, and by Alex Carrach, son of Alexander of Lochaber. The exiled James Stewart, Murdoch's son, had been given refuge by Donald Balloch and might have proved a useful tool as a figurehead for the revolt; his early death, however, cut short his participation.

The king was swift to retaliate; summoning forces, he advanced into Lochaber where a tense confrontation ensued. It had been one thing for Donald of the Isles to defy the regent, Albany, but quite another for his son to withstand the potency of the royal standard. Alexander's position became hopeless when several of his allies – the Mackenzies (no friends to the Lordship), the Camerons and Clan Chattan – defected.[15] Alexander was constrained to submit and, though his life was spared, he was taken south for imprisonment behind the isolated walls of grim Tantallon (a Douglas hold on the coast of Lothian) in the custody of the Earl of Angus.

Alexander's failure did not end the rebellion; Donald Balloch and Alexander Carrach maintained their bitter defiance. The king was prepared to entrust operations to his justiciar north of the Forth, the ageing Earl of Mar, who now found himself opposed to the sons of the men he had fought twenty years before. In September 1431 Mar, with the Earl of Caithness, led a royal army into Lochaber. They made camp by the old Comyn fortress of Inverlochy Castle,[16] while Carrach skulked in the hills around. Mar sent a commanded party of Frasers, led by their chief, Lord Lovat, to take up Sunart and Ardnamurchan.

Donald Balloch had summoned a muster on the island of Carna in Loch Sunart, where the Irish contingents were swelled by the arrival of MacIain of Ardnamurchan and Alan MacAlan of Moidart. Hugh Macdonald describes the young Donald Balloch, no more than eighteen at the time, who:

> …gathered all those who faithfully adhered to Macdonald's interest, came to Carna, an island in Loch Sunart, where meeting with the laird of Ardnamurchan, Allan son to Allan of Moidart, and his brother Ranald Bain, for these were the most principal men of the name, who were with them, picked out the best of their men to the number of 600, mostly gentlemen and freeholders, and came in their galleys to Invershippinish two miles south of Inverlochy.[17]

The Islesmen rowed over to the mainland and landed a couple of miles south of Inverlochy. Alexander Carrach and his bowmen were harassing the flanks of the royal army; this time the veteran Mar seems to have been caught unawares. The Islesmen charged home on the other flank, utterly routing the royalists, whose score of dead and wounded was said to have been as high as 900. Mar, fighting valiantly as ever, was again wounded, and though he escaped the field he was obliged to skulk in the heather for some days before rescue.[18]

Flush with triumph, Donald Balloch wreaked vengeance on the Mackenzie lands in Lochaber. Stung by the severity of the reverse, the king found Parliament unenthusiastic about voting further funds for the continuance of the war, though he was successful in raising an expedition, which advanced as far as Dunstaffnage. Here all the leading rebels, with the unsurprising exception of Donald Balloch, submitted. Those who did appear were quick to blame their absent leader for the whole affair and some sources assert the king ordered the deaths of 300 of Donald's men. Hugh Macdonald denies this, and whether such a rash of executions did take place remains questionable.

The Mackenzies received lands from Alexander Carrach as compensation for their losses and some time afterwards Hugh Boy, the chief of the Ulster O'Neills, made James a present of a severed head advertised as that of Donald Balloch. Quite who this unfortunate actually was is unknown, but Donald Balloch's head remained firmly attached to his shoulders for many years to come, nor was he done with plaguing the Stewart kings.[19]

One beneficiary of the aftermath of the battle of Inverlochy was Alexander of the Isles. The humiliation of the royal army and the king's inability to secure sufficient funds for protracted campaigning led him to the conclusion that the only effective solution was to reach a workable compromise with Alexander. Consequently he was freed, pardoned and subsequently appointed as justiciar after Mar's death. His mother was kept in genteel captivity at Incholm, under the benevolent gaze of the abbot, the chronicler Walter Bower. The further incentive of Ross may also have been offered, for Alexander begins to style himself as Earl of Ross around this time.

The rule of James I was cut short by his assassination at the Dominican priory of Perth in 1437. His murderers were led by the septuagenarian Earl of Atholl, the king's last surviving uncle, to whom the crown would descend if James's young son failed to reach maturity. Atholl's own son had predeceased him and his heir was his grandson, Sir Robert Stewart. The Grahams had joined the conspiracy because the king had stripped Malise Graham, a great-grandson of Robert II, of his earldom of Strathearn. He had received Menteith in compensation but this did not deflect the Grahams' enmity.

James was butchered by a gang of conspirators who entered the undefended priory at night. Ironically, the king had selected Perth as his principal seat because he found the city well placed to facilitate governance of the north and west. The story is a dramatic one: a servant who raised the alarm was swiftly silenced, and the king levered up the floorboards of his chamber to seek sanctuary in the undercroft below. When the murderers found him he fought them bare-handed until he fell beneath a relentless fury of thrusts. The queen valiantly trying to save her husband was also injured.

If the killers hoped to profit from their crime, they were fatally mistaken. The vengeance wreaked upon them, inspired by the queen's revulsion, was notably savage – both Atholl and Sir Robert Graham were tortured and mutilated before finally meeting a traitor's death.

James I had dealt harshly and by no means impartially with his Highland subjects; his vision of a united realm clashed with their inherent tribalism. His concept of a strong, centralised monarchy was at odds with their stubborn independence. His attitude to the Islesmen shows a level of impatience, even contempt, for the Gaels, who were to be treated as criminals rather than an accepted minority. James was a fervent believer in the rule of law as an essential element in a properly regulated society. His reign witnessed a flood of new statutes and an attempt to impose a single legal code that would overreach custom, baronial and tribal precedent. To this end, he anticipated the Court of Star Chamber in England by establishing a supreme court, staffed by royal appointees, from which there was no appeal. In due course, this important addition became the Court of Session.

The type of Scotland that James I envisaged had no place in it for any elements of separatism or for any peculiar culture distinct from the model of Anglo Norman feudalism. He was obliged, finally, to concede that the monarchy was not yet strong enough to extend its sway fully over the west. The compromise he achieved with Alexander was proof of this. It is questionable if this could have been a lasting rapprochement;

the very existence of the Lord of the Isles as a virtually free prince was a bar to a united realm.

In the immediate aftermath of the Lochaber expedition, Parliament had enacted that all of those magnates with holdings in the north and west, 'fornent the ylis',[20] were to provide galleys with an oar for each four marks in land value. These were to be ready for a spring campaign in 1431, on pain of half a mark to the king for each oar.[21] James clearly perceived that to enforce his will in the west he would need an adequate fleet.

While making steady assaults on the power and independence of the Lord of the Isles, the Crown frequently exposed its own weaknesses. The eventual collapse of the Lordship after 1493 ushered in an era of lawlessness exceeding anything seen since the days of the Vikings: 'the Age of Forays'. The Crown was simply not in a position to take the place of a strong, local lordship to which the chiefs were bound by blood and custom.[22]

The minority of James II removed the strong hand of an independent-minded king and Alexander flourished in the interregnum. As justiciar north of the Forth he wielded considerable authority, dispensing justice from Inverness, rebuilt after his earlier arson. He appears to have developed an understanding with the powerful Douglas kindred, and even forgave the Mackintoshes for their defection and hostility at Lochaber. The Camerons he could not excuse, harrying them to the extent that Donald Dubh Cameron had to flee to Ireland.

Alexander's rehabilitation and the minority of James II saw the power of the Lordship reach its apogee but, in so doing, move its axis from west to east, Easter Ross being found more congenial. Alexander issued many of his charters from Dingwall or Inverness, but this was feudal not clan territory; he exercised lordship but without affinity. For the Lords of the Isles to prefer the east coast to the west was to spurn the very fountain of their hereditary power, a trend that Alexander's son John continued.

In March 1445 the Lord of the Isles entered into a band or compact with the Douglases and the Earl of Crawford. Such indentures were far from uncommon and did not necessarily imply any hint of treasonable association. While James II was a minor, the pawn of contending factions, the matter was of little consequence, but as he grew to manhood James 'of the fiery face'[23] came to bitterly resent the vast power wielded by the Douglas affinity.

Alexander died in 1449 at his castle of Dingwall and was buried at Rosemarkie in Easter Ross – a break with family tradition, his forbears all having been interred on Iona. He left three sons: John, the eldest, now succeeded him and Celestine, the second son, received lands in Lochalsh and Lochbroom in Ross, exercising feudal lordship over the confiscated Cameron lands by Locheil in Lochaber. The youngest boy, Hugh, became the founder of Macdonald of Sleat.

John of the Isles remains something of an enigma; Hugh Macdonald asserts that he was 'a meek and modest man... more fitting to be a church-man than to command so many irregular tribes of people'.[24] While still in his teens and being advised by the irrepressible Donald Balloch, he contracted a marriage with Elizabeth, the daughter of Sir James Livingstone. Although pre-eminent among the young king's advisors, Livingstone was something of a parvenu, his daughter hardly a fitting match for the illustrious Lord of the Isles.

It is possible that the king, under Livingstone's influence, favoured the alliance and may have led John to believe he would profit thereby. If promises were made, they were never kept and the Lord of the Isles very quickly came to repent of his bargain and rue the marriage, which proved to be an extremely unhappy one for both parties.[25]

The regency court of the young king was deeply factional. In November 1440 the young Earl of Douglas and his brother dined in the king's presence at Edinburgh Castle. A the end of the meal both of the youths were seized, probably on the orders of Sir William Crichton, and, after the hurried sham of a trial, were speedily convicted of treason and both executed forthwith. Dining with James II was to prove a dangerous experience for Black Douglas!

When Livingstone fell from power in the early 1450s he fled to the protection of his powerful son-in-law, who was persuaded to raise the flag of defiance on his behalf. James II could not at this stage afford to risk alienating the Lord of the Isles. He was already flexing the royal muscles against the overmighty Douglas in the south-west. When trouble flared, John instructed Donald Balloch to seize and hold Urquhart and Inverness while Ruthven in Badenoch was taken and slighted. The two captured castles were entrusted to Livingstone's governorship. He was to remain in possession for three years.

The young and headstrong eighth Earl Douglas accepted the king's invitation to dine at Stirling in 1452, despite the unfortunate precedent.[26] This dinner proved as bloody as the last. The king apparently had some personal affection for the earl, but when, after supper, Douglas refused to repudiate the agreement with Crawford and Macdonald, James flew into a drink-fuelled range and struck the first blow. His attendants rushed in to complete the bloody work.

This was an act of war, and the feud with the Douglases smouldered until the dead earl's brothers were decisively defeated at Arkinholm in 1455, by a royal army led, with fitting irony, by the 'Red' Douglas, Earl of Angus! The ninth Earl Douglas, fleeing the wrack of his family's fortunes, sought the protection of John of the Isles. Donald Balloch had led a fleet of 100 galleys in a lightning descent on the coast of Ayrshire. Satisfying and profitable as this expedition undoubtedly was, such aimless freebooting served no strategic purpose. Douglas fled to the surer sanctuary of the English court and John was left to deal with the king.

For all of his apparent treachery, John escaped very lightly. The king was still not strong enough to try conclusions. Retaining virtually all of his offices, John finally surrendered both Urquhart and Inverness, though he was immediately granted a life tenancy of each.[27] Even his father-in-law, Livingstone, was rehabilitated.

For the remainder of James II's short life relations appeared cordial; with the Douglas skulking in England, the king needed John as an ally. The battle of Arkinholm in Scotland was followed by the outbreak of that series of dynastic conflicts in England later to be known as the Wars of the Roses. The battle of St Albans in 1455 was followed by an uneasy calm before more fighting at Blore Heath and then, in 1460, at Northampton, when the Yorkists appeared to have gained the upper hand and controlled the person of Henry VI.

James, planning to succeed where his father failed, laid siege to Roxburgh, one of the great border fortresses, in 1460. John of the Isles led a body of some 3,000 retainers to campaign with the king: 'all armed in the highland fashion, with habergeons, bows and axes, and promised to the king, if he pleased to pass any further in the bounds of England, that he and his company should pass a large mile afore the rest of the host, and take upon them the first press and dint of the battle'.[28] John was not called upon to make good his offer, for the king, a great advocate of the new science of gunnery, was killed when one of his siege guns burst, while delivering a cannonade to mark the arrival of the queen in camp.

With commendable resolution, the widowed queen, Marie de Gueldres, persuaded the magnates to continue the siege until the garrison, commanded by Lord Fauconberg, surrendered. The castle was then slighted. In England, the year 1460 closed with the death of the Duke of York in battle at Wakefield and the next year opened with a series of bloody encounters. Queen Margaret and the Duke of Somerset bested Warwick the Kingmaker at the second battle of St Albans, but the Welsh Lancastrians were defeated by Edward, Earl of March beneath the parhelion at Mortimer's Cross. The two sides squared up for a conclusion and the decisive battle was fought on Palm Sunday at Towton.

Fleeing to Northumberland with what forces she could salvage from the disaster, Margaret of Anjou was prepared, in her reckless desperation, to trade the two great border bastions of Berwick and Carlisle as the price of Scottish support. The Regency Council was split; there was some support for Lancaster but also a general wariness. The wiser heads in council saw little advantage in Scotland, with no adult monarch to lead her, becoming embroiled in a civil war in England, particularly on behalf of the faction that was already defeated. In the event, Berwick was handed over and remained in Scottish hands until recaptured by Richard of Gloucester, some twenty years later. The citizens of Carlisle proved a good deal less amenable and barred their gates against the Scots, whose attempt at leaguer was soon seen off by Lord Montagu, the Kingmaker's able brother.

The Earl of March, now crowned Edward IV and advised by the renegade Douglas, was persuaded of an opportunity to intervene in Scotland by seeking an alliance with the Lord of the Isles. Douglas was empowered to enter into negotiations with John of the Isles and talks began on 19 October 1461 at Ardtornish. With the earl were Sir William Wells, Dr Kingscote and John Stanley. Ranald Bain (John Mor Tanister's younger son) and Duncan, Archdeacon of Ross spoke for John.

The fruit of these clandestine discussions was the rather preposterous sounding Treaty of Westminster-Ardtornish, sealed on 13 February 1462 after a final series of negotiations when John's ambassadors travelled to the English court. To give gravitas to the talks, the English Crown was represented by the bishop of Durham, the Earl of Worcester, Lord Wenlock, the prior of St John's and the Keeper of the Privvy Seal.

The terms of the accord were that, in return for English military assistance, John would repudiate his loyalty to the young James III. In return for control of all of the country north of the Forth, he would become Edward's vassal. Douglas was to benefit to a similar extent in the southwest. Until full partition was achieved, the Scottish lords were to be paid an annual compensation from the English exchequer:

The stipulated salaries were to the Earl [John] £200.00 sterling annually in time of war, and one hundred marks in time of peace; to Donald Balloch £40.00 and to John, his son £20.00 in time of war, and in times of peace half these sums respectively.[29]

At first glance John's involvement in so wild a scheme reeks of cardinal folly. He was entering into a treasonable alliance with England, brokered by a notorious traitor. Edward did not have the resources to invade Scotland; his purpose was to create a dangerous distraction that would cause the Scots to rethink any dalliance with the house of Lancaster. From the king of England's perspective the thing made perfect sense; he was fomenting discord in the Scottish polity and sponsoring, at little or no cost, a powerful 'fifth column'.

To understand John's motives, it is necessary to dispense with any thoughts of nationalism. Although Scotland had existed as a nation since the century before the Wars of Independence, and although the powerful tone of the Declaration of Arbroath in 1320 speaks emotively of nationhood, this should not necessarily be confused with patriotism. John of the Isles thought in terms of the Lordship and Clan Donald; the wider concept of nationalism had little to offer. His duty was to his kindred and affinity and the hereditary right of his titles. From the days of Somerled the Islesmen had sought to resist the encroachment of royal authority; to him Westminster-Ardtornish was but a further manifestation of this.

It was Donald Balloch who, in 1463, was once again chosen to bear the standard of rebellion, seconded by John's illegitimate and warlike son, Angus Og. The fiery cross went around and Inverness, always first to bear the brunt, was taken. John, as Earl of Ross, issued proclamations to the effect that he was assuming regal power in the royal burghs of Inverness and Nairn and that the whole of the northern lands were to give their absolute obedience to Angus Og as his nominee, on pain of death, and to pay to him all customs dues hitherto payable to the Crown.

The Macdonalds persisted in this rebellion for nearly a year, with Angus Og collecting Crown monies and adding to his income by levying blackmail. The Frasers, with the Macraes and Forbeses, took exception to Clan Donald looting their way through the Aird and came out to fight. The Islesmen were driven off with loss and, as the Fraser historian remarks with grim satisfaction: 'the Macdonells came no more here to try their vassalage upon the Frasers'.[30]

The extent of John's treachery was probably not fully appreciated until the Scots themselves came to treat with Edward IV's commissioners in the spring of 1464. The Lancastrians made one last desperate attempt to bar the passage of the envoys as they passed through Northumberland, by taking a stand at Hedgeley Moor against Montagu's force hurrying to meet them. The Yorkists brushed them aside and in the same month Montagu capitalised on this success by utterly defeating Somerset again, this time decisively, at Hexham.

Most of the Lancastrian leaders were captured in the rout and were made to pay the full price of failure. Once a formal truce between England and Scotland was negotiated, any residual hopes the few surviving Lancastrians might have entertained were dashed, and at the same time John of the Isles was abandoned. Douglas's projected invasion had ended in a near farcical-debacle and in his capture.[31]

The question has to be asked as to whether Edward IV simply and conveniently forgot about John of the Isles and the earlier treaty, or whether he was minded to negotiate assurances of clemency. This may have been the case, for John came out of the affair relatively unscathed. Part of his salvation was that James III remained a minor and the court continued to be beset by factions. He was obliged to admit only that the seizure and retention of Crown monies had been an illegal act. The matter of his abortive rebellion was thus concluded, but not by any means forgotten.

John of the Isles was not the man his father and grandfather had been. He was by nature, most probably, lacking in aggression and was thus prey to the dangerous counsels of hotheads such as Donald Balloch, whose instincts owed more to the rough and tumble of the Norse Gael past than to the intricacies of fifteenth-century diplomacy. Equally, by failing to win new lands John found it impossible to placate all of the factions within his complex affinity. Despite the external pressures of the second half of the century, it was to be internal dissent which finally brought the Lordship down.

As if the failure of his alliance with Douglas and the English Crown was not sufficient to preoccupy John of the Isles, he also had to cope with the final breakdown of his marriage. At some point in 1463–1464, Elizabeth petitioned the Pope to admonish John for his presumably flagrant adultery and alienation. The woman in question is unknown but may have been the mother of Angus Og. Possibly in fear of her life, Elizabeth fled to seek sanctuary at court.

John's next dispute was with Donald Balloch, who had served him loyally these many years. Perhaps he blamed his cousin for the debacle of Westminster-Ardtornish, though the immediate cause of the rupture appears to have been increasing tension over land tenure. The *Annals of Ulster* record that in 1465 Donald's son Angus was killed in a fracas with some of John's retainers. In the following year the Lord of the Isles granted lands in Lochaber to Duncan Mackintosh of Clan Chattan, despite the fact that the Keppoch Macdonalds had already laid claim to part of them. In 1469, by attempting to grant estates on Skye to his younger brother Hugh, John offended the powerful Macleods. His own son and heir, Angus Og, objected to gains made by the Macleans in Morvern. It was a case of trying to please all while satisfying none.[32]

By 1475 James III had come of age and Edward IV was fully occupied with plans for a projected invasion of France. The Scottish Crown was therefore well placed to bring its most illustrious and troublesome vassal to heel. John was summoned to attend Parliament and there to answer for his numerous acts of alleged treason. The list of accusations was impressive, going back nearly quarter of a century and including Westminster-Ardtornish. The Lord of the Isles failed to appear and his titles were duly forfeited on 1 December 1475.

If he thought he could skulk in the west and ride out the storm, he had again miscalculated. The king instructed Colin Campbell, first Earl of Argyll, to mount a punitive expedition, and a further commission was issued to Gordon, Earl of Huntly, who by the end of March 1476 had successfully taken Dingwall. The net was closing. John had no talent for generalship; he had alienated Donald Balloch, his most experienced captain, and may already by this time have lost the respect of Angus Og. He had no choice but to submit to the king's pleasure.

The terms, given the extent of John's perfidy, do not appear at first glance unduly harsh. He was stripped of the earldom of Ross, save for Skye, which he was permitted to retain; the rump reverted to the Crown by direct annexation. He also lost lands in Knapdale and Kintyre. He also nominally surrendered all his other estates, which were then re-granted to him by order of the Crown, and he was formally created a Baron Banrent and peer of Parliament, with the title 'Lord of the Isles'.

The succession rights of both Angus Og and his brother John, despite the taint of bastardy, were recognised. The loss was far greater than it appeared; John was no longer a Norse Gael prince of the line of Somerled, holding his lands by ancient right and supported by the broadswords of his kin. He was now a purely feudal magnate whose estates belonged to the Crown and could thus be forfeited at any time Parliament so chose.[33]

If John was able to accept the full measure of his humiliation, Angus Og could not. Resentment over the confiscation of Ross and the other lost acres festered (in spite of this, it is possible that Angus married a daughter of the Earl of Argyll at about this time). For him, the loss and humiliation was too bitter a pill; his father's tame surrender also rankled and some time in 1481 Angus Og led a rebellion of the Islesmen. By this time he had effectively marginalised John, who, according to Hugh Macdonald, had been unceremoniously turfed out of his house wearing only his nightshirt! In this he appears to have had the support of the various septs of Clan Donald, equally frustrated at John's impotence, but the rest of the affinity supported their ousted lord.

John had already been summoned before Parliament to answer fresh allegations of treason in 1478 and was freshly accused three years later when Angus Og made a bid to seize Knapdale by force and captured Castle Sween. In both instances John managed to extricate himself by skilful diplomacy, but the plain fact was he was no longer in control. Angus Og was making moves to recover Ross, and this brought him into direct conflict with the parallel ambitions of the Mackenzies.

In an earlier effort to bring about a cessation of the feud, John of the Isles had betrothed his daughter, Margaret, to Kenneth Mackenzie, the chief's son and heir. The union was not a success; the bride was not to her new husband's liking, being among other failings apparently blind in one eye. Having partially occupied Easter Ross, Angus Og held Christmas there, inviting all to share his hospitality. Kenneth Mackenzie duly attended, but without his wife, the host's half-sister. This of itself was a grave breach of protocol – both a slight and a provocation.

Worse was to follow. Angus had appointed as his chamberlain one of the Macleans of Duart; a dispute arose, possibly over the order of precedence, always a tricky matter. Mackenzie and Maclean exchanged words and then blows. Who threw the first punch is uncertain, but Kenneth, a man of great physical strength, soon felled his opponent. The Macdonalds now rose in anger to defend their man and Kenneth, with his own followers, was constrained to beat a speedy retreat. Driven outside, the Mackenzies sought shelter at the next gentleman's dwelling.

Kenneth, to avoid the shame of having to admit he had spent Christmas as a virtual beggar beneath another man's roof, persuaded his host to adopt the clan surname![34] To formalise this agreement, Kenneth next journeyed to attend the bishop of Ross, his host's feudal superior, and effectively leased the estate from him to the tenant, now become a sub-tenant of Mackenzie.

Angus Og, who could have let matters rest, responded to this per-ceived provocation by demanding the land now be surrendered to him, presumably as Mackenzie's feudal superior. Kenneth refused, and went further by repudiating the marriage contract and sending poor one-eyed and by now heavily pregnant Margaret back to her family, seated on a one-eyed horse, led by a one-eyed servant with a one-eyed dog! It is said the unfortunate young woman did not survive the shame.

Having virtually declared war, Kenneth allied himself and his kin-dred to the swelling ranks of Angus's enemies; these included the Frasers, Mackays, Brodies and Rosses, mustering under the banners of the Earl of Atholl. Angus was ready and the two sides met in open battle at Lagabraad in Ross, where the long swords of Clan Donald decimated their enemies, leaving some 500 and more dead on the field. Despite the considerable tactical victory he had won, Angus Og realised that the odds in Easter Ross were too great and he subsequently withdrew into the west.

Angus did not enjoy the support of the whole Macdonald affinity and both his father-in-law, Argyll, and Atholl, doubtless smarting from his bloody repulse, were swift to exploit the growing divide. Ranged against the various septs of Clan Donald was an alliance of Maclean of Duart, Macleod of Harris and Lewis together with Macneil. Led by Maclean, the disaffected mustered a powerful fleet on the Mull side of the Sound, at a location now called Bloody Bay. Angus Og had taken station on the north side of the Ardnamurchan Peninsula where contrary winds kept him penned. The Macdonalds languished at anchor for five weeks until the wind changed direction; they then hoisted sail to round the penin-sula and offer battle at sea.

As his fleet proceeded over the Sound, Angus's lookouts spotted an enemy squadron under Maclean of Ardgour, their defiant pennants streaming in the wind. Seeing an opportunity to strike a blow, Angus gave the order to attack. Maclean of Duart, perceiving his kinsman's peril, led the rest of his fleet to join in the engagement, which now became general. This was a battle from the great days of Somerled, long and bloody; eventually Angus gained the upper hand and the other clans were scattered. It was a great Macdonald victory – but there is little honour in what was, to all intents and purposes, a civil war. Hugh Macdonald again provides the detail:

> ...the rest of the faction, seeing themselves in danger at least of losing their galleys, thought best to enter their harbour. Macdonald coming as swiftly as he could, accompanied by Donald Gallich of Sleat, Austin's son [his first cousin] and Ranald Bain, laird of Mudort's son, the last of whom grappled side to side with Macleod of Harris's galley. There was one called Edmond More Obrian along with Ranald Bain, who thrust the blade of an oar in below the stern post of Macleod's galley, between it and the rudder, which prevented the galley from being steered. The galley of the heir of Torkill of the Lewis, with all his men was taken, and himself mortally wounded with two arrows, whereof he died soon after at Dunvegan. Angus Og and Allan, Laird of Mudort, attacked Macleod and took him prisoner with a great slaughter of his men. Angus Og would have hanged Maclean immediately had he not been prevented by the laird of Mudort saying, he would have none to bicker with if Maclean was gone...[35]

Though the records of the period are rather vague, it would appear that while Angus Og was diverted by his naval campaign Atholl launched a raid on Islay and kidnapped his infant son, Donald Dubh ('Dark Donald'). The child was held prisoner in his grandfather Argyll's hold of Inch Chonail Castle, an isolated tower standing on an island in Loch Awe. Angus descended with fire and sword on the earl's lands. Both Atholl and his countess were dragged from sanctuary but Angus, repenting of this sacrilege and offering penance, released them unharmed. There appears to have been no exchange of prisoners, as surely could have been negotiated.[36]

Militarily Angus was in the ascendancy; he was able to take possession of Inverness and establish a measure of uneasy control over Ross. The early 1480s were a difficult time for James III, who had succeeded in alienating the majority of the magnates. A great patron of the arts, James was unmilitary and preferred the company of his coterie of base-born favourites, relationships that were tainted with the suggestion of homosexuality.

When finally bestirred to counter Gloucester's invasion and siege of Berwick in 1482, the king unwisely took his posse of courtiers along. The frustrations of the nobility boiled over at Lauder, where there was a prolific cull orchestrated by Angus, the unfortunate favourites being hanged from Lauder Bridge. A virtual prisoner of the disaffected magnates, and with the English able to occupy Edinburgh unopposed, James was in no position to intervene in the north and west.

Angus Og now had problems of his own. Kenneth Mackenzie remained a mortal foe and he had made a bitter enemy of his cousin's wife. Clanranald of Moidart was married to a daughter of Rory 'the Black', the tutor to young Macleod of Lewis. The unscrupulous Rory had schemed to cheat the lad of his rightful inheritance. Angus, quite rightly, it seems had intervened to frustrate the theft and thereby created another enemy!

What follows has the ring of a Jacobean tragedy, worthy of Webster or Ford at their most bloodily creative:

> There was an Irish harper by the name of Art O'Carby, of the county of Monaghan in Ireland, who was often at Macdonald's and, falling in love with Mackenzie's daughter, he became almost mad in his amours. Mackenzie, seeing him in that mood, promised him his daughter provided he would put Macdonald to death, and made him swear never to reveal the secret, This fellow being afterwards in his cups, and playing upon his harp used to sing the following verse, composed by himself in the Irish language... meaning that the rider of the dapple horse was in danger of his life (for Macdonald always rode such a one), if there was poison in his long knife which he caled Gallfit. As Macdonald went to bed one night, there was none in the room along with him but John Cameron, brother to Ewan, Lorch of Locheill, and Macmurrich the poet. The harper rose in the night time, when he perceived Macdonald was asleep, and cut his throat for which he was apprehended, but never confessed that he was employed by any body so to do, although there were several jewels found upon him, which were well known to have belonged formerly to Mackenzie and the lady of Muidort. The harper was drawn after horses till his limbs were torn asunder.[37]

With the death of Angus Og in 1490, any real hope of a sustained revival in the fortunes of the Lordship faded. James III had been dead for two years; his relations with the nobility had always been fractious and the king was murdered by an unknown assailant as he lay wounded after the rout of his forces at Sauchieburn. His son, James IV, was now king and proved considerably more masterful and dynamic than his unfortunate parent.

In the Isles, Angus Og was succeeded by Alexander of Lochalsh, a nephew of John of the Isles. Angus's son, Donald Dubh, may still have been a prisoner of his grandfather, who appears to have asserted the boy was illegitimate. The fact that Alexander succeeded may be evidence to support this. It is also possible that Donald Dubh was not kidnapped until some years later, in 1501, when he was rescued by Macdonald of Glencoe. After a brief taste of liberty has was recaptured and held as a state prisoner, until his second escape over forty years later![38]

Whether Alexander saw himself as tutor to Donald Dubh or as Angus Og's successor remains unclear, although the latter seems more probable. Like his murdered predecessor, he sought the means to re-establish control of Ross, which must have slipped in the wake of the murder. Alexander had at least a foothold in Wester Ross, as he had inherited lands around Lochalsh from his uncle.

Holding an initial muster of his Islesmen in Lochaber, Alexander collected the Camerons and Macdonalds of Keppoch on the march; he then continued his advance through Glen Spean into Badenoch where he was reinforced by Mackintosh, now at feud with Keppoch! Inverness fell once again and Alexander installed his own garrison, before leading the rump of his army into Cromarty. Having dealt, as he imagined, with any likely resistance, he discharged a number of his fighters and took the remainder on a *chevauchée* into the Mackenzie country of Strathconan.

Kenneth Mackenzie was not the man to refuse such a challenge and he mustered as many of his name as he was able; nonetheless, Macdonald still enjoyed a comfortable superiority in numbers. It was to be, at least in part, a later version of Harlaw. On a Sunday morning, having roasted a Mackenzie congregation, the Islesmen were spread along the hills surrounding the Strath of Conin, a large natural amphitheatre. Mackenzie was outnumbered by at least three to one; Alexander, with fatal overconfidence, did not believe he would dare such odds. He had misjudged his man.

The ensuing battle of Blar na Pairc was fought out over a maze of peat hags and mosses. Kenneth deployed his archers in the rear as an ambush and led the van toward the waiting Macdonalds. His aim was to execute a fake withdrawal and lead the Islesmen back toward his concealed bowmen. Suspecting this might be the case, Gillespie, Alexander's brother, advocated a cautious response. But the new Lord of the Isles would have none of it; roundly accusing his sibling of faintheartedness.[39] He ordered the charge, Maclean of Loch Buy leading the van. In the difficult terrain the attack lost impetus and foundered. The Mackenzies held the charge long enough for the ambush party to put in a decisive flank attack. It was a rout; Alexander's Islesmen broke and ran, many drowning in the river Conan.[40]

It may have been this debacle that prompted James IV to finally forfeit the Lordship which he did in 1493, bringing the great days of Clan Donald to an end. The Lordship of the Isles ended far more with a whimper than a bang; the dispossessed John ended his life as a pathetic royal pensioner. Alexander was defeated a second time by a coalition of Mackenzies and Munros, but he retired south to try and raise a fresh army from the Macdonald septs. His efforts were cut short by Macian of Ardnamurchan who was already a royal collaborator (he had captured Sir John Macdonald of Islay and his sons), who surprised and murdered Alexander on Oransay.

It was a fitting irony that the last effective Macdonald Lord of the Isles should die by the treacherous hand of a kinsman. Macian was not just motivated by the desire to win royal approbation and advancement; he, like the other cadet branches, had no wish to see a powerful Lordship survive – they had more to gain from the Crown, which had already parcelled out lands previously held by Angus Og to them.

Despite the fall of the Lordship, Clan Donald was not likely to fade into obscurity. As late as 1545, for his final campaign, Donald Dubh was still able to muster 180 galleys and 4,000 broadswords on Islay.[41] After 1493 James IV, who styled his son 'Prince of Scotland and the Isles', was obliged to mount five separate expeditions. The Scottish Parliaments of 1504, 1506 and 1509 were all taken up with disturbances in the west. Between 1494 and 1545 there were six serious uprisings. After his father's death at Flodden and his own troubled minority, James V still failed to completely subdue the Islesmen:

> The entrenched resistance of the Lordship throughout these three reigns is a salutary reminder that the Stewart monarchy was not always 'laissez-faire'; in the isles it was at once at its most centralist and its most unsuccessful.[42]

Having disposed of the Lordship, the Crown had to seek reliance on other strong local magnates. The obvious tools were Argyll and Huntly, though both failed from time to time to meet royal expectations.

In 1531 the fourth Earl of Argyll was sacked for his signal failure to produce lawful obedience. The Campbells were desperate to fill the void but could never, despite their best endeavours, attain the prestige of the Lordship. Their position was difficult; on the one hand they were sworn to uphold the edicts of a centralised state but on the other they were expected to champion the local interest. The two priorities rarely coincided.

The final comment upon the Lordship has to be the popular epithet for the era of near-anarchy which ensued. Finlaggan was abandoned, if for no other reason than that it was indefensible, and from now on a gentleman would need to look to his ramparts. The real legacy of the forfeiture of 1493 was the *Linn nan Creach* – the Age of Forays – and that is another story.

Glossary

Aketon	a quilted form of 'soft' armour (derived from the Arabic for cotton)
Arbalest	a form of crossbow spanned by a windlass for maximum velocity
Arming cap	padded fabric cap worn beneath a mail 'coif' or iron helm
Aventail	a section of mail attached to the lower rim of a helmet to protect the neck
Ballock knife	a thin-bladed dagger with a wooden hilt fashioned to resemble the male sexual organs
Bascinet (basinet)	a conical helmet which encases the head, may be open-faced or fitted with a visor
Battle (Battail)	a division of an army
Bevor	a detachable plate defence that protected the neck and lower face
Birlinn	a Hebridean galley
Blazon	heraldic device or coat of arms
Bolt	a short thick arrow fired from a crossbow also called a 'quarrel'
Bond of manrent	a contract evidenced in writing and entered into by a magnate and his retainer, whereby the lord offered his protection in return for homage
Breast and back	the front and rear sections of a plate armour, covering the torso
Brigandine	a fabric-covered form of body armour, often sewn with small metal plates
Buckler	a small, round metal shield with raised central boss used for punching and parrying
Buannacht	an Irish term referring to free quarter for a magnate's mercenary forces
Camail	mail attached to the helm, similar to but less extensive than the aventail
Caparison	a fabric horse covering, often decorative and also padded for protection
Captain	a middle-ranking military commander; sometimes led a company or a battalion, or commanded a fixed garrison, usually of knightly status
Cateran	a mercenary Highland warrior in the service of a feudal or Gaelic magnate
Chamfron	plate armour to protect the head, neck and chest of a war horse
Clarsach	a Highland harp
Close helmet	a fitted metal helmet covering the whole head and fitted with a rounded visor
Coif	hood of chain mail to protect the head and neck
Comital	pertaining to the estates of a senior magnate (from French: *comte*)
Constable	a senior officer in a royal household responsible for military organisation
Couter	plate section covering the elbows
Danish axe	a long-handled broad-bladed fighting axe of the Vikings and Norse Gaels

Destrier	the war horse of the medieval knight
Enceinte	a defensible enclosure i.e. the walls of a castle or fortified town
Enfoeff	to grant a feudal estate
Fauld	lower section of plate body defences covering upper thighs and buttocks
Fief	a feudal estate or parcel of land, that necessary to support a single knight
Ferm toun	a medieval Scottish farm or small hamlet
Fuller	the central channel or groove in a sword blade, not intended to facilitate spilt blood but to lighten the blade
Gallowglass	a Hebridean mercenary in the service of an Irish magnate, fourteenth to late sixteenth century
Gisarme	a staff weapon with a broadly curved axe blade (with or without a hook)
Gorget	plate section protecting the neck
Greaves	plate defences, hinged at the sides covering the calves
Halberd	a staff weapon with a heavy axe blade and thrusting spike
'Halflang' sword	Scottish single-handed sword of the fifteenth century, with long double-edged blade and distinctive downward-sweeping quillons
Haubergeon	a mail shirt, shorter and lighter version of the earlier hauberk, often with short sleeves, in use from the fourteenth century
Hauberk	long-sleeved mail shirt reaching to mid-thigh, eleventh to fourteenth century
Jack	similar to a brigandine but with metal plates sewn between layers of fabric and rivet heads exposed externally in a decorative pattern
Kern(e)	Irish warrior similar to a cateran, a paid military retainer
Kettle hat	a circular metal helmet with a protective rim, fourteenth to fifteenth century
Lance	steel-tipped cavalry spear, initially used overarm, latterly couched; also refers to the basic tactical cavalry unit of the medieval period
Lochaber axe	distinctive form of Highland polearm, not known before the early sixteenth century; not to be confused with the borderers' equivalent, the 'Jeddart' axe
Maule	a wooden mallet used by archers for hammering in defensive stakes; could be employed as a handy weapon for 'bashing' armoured men at arms
Mêlée	usually refers to the mass combat between opposing cavalry once the charge has struck home
Mesnie	pertaining to the lord's household; in the military context, household knights
Mormaer	provincial governor and military commander, Pictish and early-medieval Scotland
Motte and bailey	a Norman defensive system consisting of a higher and lower mounds of earth, the latter being larger and surrounded by a timber palisade, within the domestic buildings, hall, stables, kitchen, chapel etc. The higher, conical mound was reached by a timber causeway and was topped by a defensive tower wherein the garrison, if hard pressed, could make a final stand
Palfrey	everyday horse, ridden on campaign but not into battle
Pauldron	plate defence for the front of the shoulder, from late fourteenth century onward
Pisane	a large mail 'tippet' which covered the neck and shoulders, extending to upper arms and chest

Poleaxe	a knightly staff weapon having a strong axe blade, thrusting spike and rear-mounted hammer head, for engaging armoured opponents in foot combat
Pommel	the disc or lobe-shaped metal section at the head of the sword hilt which anchored the metal tang of the blade to the handle; also important as an element of the weapon's balance or 'heft'
Quillon	the crossguard of the medieval sword, the quillons were level, sloped or curving and projected from either side of the hilt
Quillon dagger	a dagger with swept, downturned quillons used for thrusting or parrying
Rondel dagger	a long-bladed dagger with usually a thin single-edged blade and circular hilt and grips
Schiltrom	Scottish infantry formation comprising of a body of spearmen, employed both for the defensive and offensive
Scutage	a fee payable in cash as commutation of feudal service
Sergeant	professional soldier, usually from the commons and restricted to infantry; then as now a form of non-commissioned officer of lesser status than a knight or gentleman
Splint	narrow strip of iron plate used to construct defences before or as an alternative to shaped plate sections
Steel bonnet	a simple, round iron skull worn by the commons (not to be confused with the sixteenth-century burgonet which became identified with the Anglo-Scottish border reivers – 'The Steel Bonnets')
Tailzie	the entail of a legal estate (Scotland)
Tang	the thin section at the hilt end of the sword blade to which the handle or grips are secured
Targe(t)	a round wooden shield made of layers of wood bonded together and covered with a leather outer layer, decorated with studs; used for parrying and defence, and latterly often equipped with a spike to facilitate the former
Tasset	hinged thigh defences for plate armour
Vambrace	a hinged section of plate armour for the lower arms
'Wappinschaw'	a Scottish muster where men appeared and brought their arms for inspection; a form of regular drill meeting, as a rule both unpopular and poorly attended

Maps

1 Map of Scotland in the early fifteenth century showing the extent of the Lordship of the Isles and the earldom of Ross.

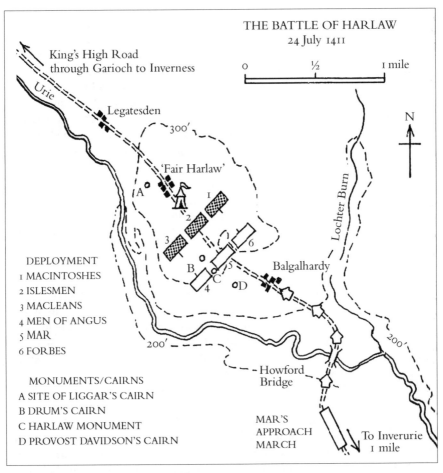

THE BATTLE OF HARLAW
24 July 1411

King's High Road
through Garioch to Inverness

0   ½   1 mile

Urie

Legatesden

N

300'

'Fair Harlaw'

A

1

2

3

6

Lochter Burn

DEPLOYMENT
1 MACINTOSHES
2 ISLESMEN
3 MACLEANS
4 MEN OF ANGUS
5 MAR
6 FORBES

B

C

4

5

D

Balgalhardy

200'

200'

MONUMENTS/CAIRNS
A SITE OF LIGGAR'S CAIRN
B DRUM'S CAIRN
C HARLAW MONUMENT
D PROVOST DAVIDSON'S CAIRN

Howford
Bridge

MAR'S
APPROACH
MARCH

To Inverurie
1 mile

2 Plan of the battlefield of Harlaw, 24 July 1411.

Appendix I
The Battlefield Today

The battlefield monument which now stands so commandingly by the roadside was designed by Dr William Kelly and was intended to be completed in time for the 500th anniversary of the fight. It was not, however, actually unveiled until three years later, on the eve of a far larger conflict that was to claim many the lives of many thousands of Scots. Intended as a tribute from the people of Aberdeen to Davidson and the three dozen burgesses who fought, the great squat tower in grey and pink granite dominates the field, leading the eye over the valley of the Urie to where the Mither Tap of Bennachie thrusts against the sky. The view at present is not enhanced by an aesthetically challenged row of pylons!

In that distant, ominous summer of 1914, a pageant commemorating the battle was staged on Coronation Day, to somewhat mixed reviews, as a contemporary newspaper account observes: 'to those who took an interest in the historical details, the procession was one of great interest... but a section of the onlookers regarded the procession as merely a grotesque display'.[1]

The 'ferm toun' of Harlaw no longer exists; the pleasant house which occupies the ground now dates from the nineteenth century, although the well which survives is said to have been that which served the original settlement. There is also a much later hamlet standing at Balhalgardy; only the old name remains. The land is essentially unchanged and yet the wide expanse of carefully cultivated fields is an entirely different prospect from the open moorland of 1411.

One of the earliest memorials erected on or close to the field is said to have been that raised by Sir Alexander Leslie to the memory of his six sons, who fell on the day. Drum's cairn has also vanished, planted, it is said, to mark the spot where Irvine and Maclean fought their sanguinary duel. The stones were most probably used, as Peter Marren suggests, in building stone dykes. The cairn may have stood a short distance north-west of the present obelisk. Provost Davidson's cairn stood some little way north-west of the present Balhalgardy and was said to commemorate the exact location where he fell.

Mention has previously been made of the prehistoric monolith called the Liggar Stone which was apparently in the immediate vicinity of Harlaw 'toun'. By the stone were interred the female dead, presumably of Donald's army, who had died on the field. No trace of this fascinating inhumation remains, for the Liggar Stone itself was subsequently moved to the Mains of Inveramsay to serve as a gatepost. A further stone structure known, rather obscurely, as Donald's Tomb, and which was constructed of four upright pillars with a horizontal capstone, was dismantled around 1800.

A most interesting museum is maintained by the City Council of Aberdeen in Provost Skene's house in the city centre. It contains among its exhibits the head of a battle axe which is said to have been dug from the field. Previously it also housed sections of plate armour said to have been worn by Provost Davidson. These tantalising fragments are no longer on display, although Dr Douglas Simpson was in no doubt they were not contemporary, belonging to a much later period.

What is sure is that Davidson's remains were interred before the altar of the chantry chapel of St Ann's Toun Kirk in the city. Sections of what may have been the tomb were excavated during subsequent alterations. The effigy of a knight which stands by the north transept of the present St Nicholas may be his (although Dr Douglas Simpson was extremely sceptical about this).

Mar himself died in late July 1435 and was buried in Greyfriars church in Inverness. The rather battered remains of a stone effigy which survives on the wall of the ruined church may possibly be his; the tomb itself is long vanished, destroyed in the iconoclastic holocaust of the Reformation.[2] Bower wrote him a fitting epitaph:

> He was a man of great achievement, who in his youth was wholly untamed, and a leader of cateran. But later he came to himself and being changed into another man, peaceably ruled the whole country north of the Mounth. He was a man of immense wealth and vast expenditure, and his name was renowned in many lands.[3]

All in all, a pretty fair assessment; he succeeded where his father had failed, and he is credited as the victor of Harlaw. Certainly without his guiding hand the battle would not have been fought, for he rather than Donald was its architect. Whether the bloodletting was necessary or proper is a matter of conjecture but he was hailed as the saviour of the Lowlands. His victory, however pyrrhic, caused the Highland host to recoil and frustrated the Lord of the Isles's great design. Had the battle not been fought Donald would have asserted his grip on Ross, which might have proven unshakeable. Without that victory, the Lord of the Isles would never be secure in the earldom.

It is said that the spot where Sir Alexander Irvine of Drum issued final instructions to his followers concerning the provisions of his will and arrangements for his son's forthcoming marriage, before hastening to the field, is now marked by the Drum Stone. This stands within a circular enclosure adjacent to the present road at Auchrone, Skene. The inscription simply reads 'Drum Stone – 1411 – Harlaw' and on a clear day both Drum Tower and the battlefield are visible.

In the *New Statistical Account* of the parish of Chapel o' Garioch there is a report that:

> In the year 1837, when the tenant of Harlaw was trenching a piece of barren ground, about a quarter of a mile to the north of the field of battle, he dug up the bones of about

twelve human bodies...The place in which they were found was a trench about 3½ feet deep, 4 feet wide and 12 feet in length.[4]

It would be truly fascinating if these remains could have been subjected to the same degree of forensic examination, using modern techniques, as the skeletons disinterred from Towton battlefield in 1996!

Today the Bass of Inverurie remains the perfect example of a motte and bailey fortification. The modern cemetery encloses it and access is gained through the well-tended graveyard, an appropriate reminder perhaps of the events of 24 July 1411. The road through Inverurie, the B9001, bisects the town, a ribbon development, little of which predates the nineteenth century. Once across the Urie (the present crossing is several hundred yards east of Howford Bridge), the road begins to climb toward the plateau on which the battle was fought.

A minor road branches left after about a mile and leads via present-day Balhalgardy to the monument, following roughly the same line as the King's Highway did in the fifteenth century. The panorama of the battlefield itself is unspoilt, though it does require some exercise of the imagination to strip away the inroads of modern intensive agriculture and restore the plain to its more natural state. Only then might we envisage the sprawl of Donald's encampment spewing forth a torrent of armed men, bright in saffron and plaid, the morning sunlight glancing from burnished mail and keen-edged blades.

The road heads north-west for half a mile or so, crossing the field before reaching the T-junction at modern Harlaw. The right-hand fork leads toward Legatesden and the Mains of Inveramsay; the left twists down from the rim of the plateau to Inveramsay. The strength of Donald's position astride the plateau is immediately visible. In the early fifteenth century both the valleys of the Urie and Lochter Burn would be wetter and marshier, securing both flanks. The great natural strength of the position is best appreciated when viewed from a distance, looking eastward from Balquhain Main on the minor road that heads to Chapel of Garioch.

The effigy of Sir Gilbert of Greenlaw still rests in ruined Kinkell church, which stands some four miles south of the field and is reached via the B993. Leave Inverurie behind, passing the cemetery and the Bass and crossing the Don by a picturesque hump-backed bridge; turn right a little while thereafter onto a minor road which leads to the ruined chapel. There you may see the knight, perhaps the most tangible memorial of all to the battle.

> But when the King Edward heard say
> How Neil the Bruce held Kildrummy
> Against his son so stalwartly:
> He gatherit a great chevelry,
> And toward Scotland went in by [haste].
> *John Barbour*[5]

Kildrummy still stands, some thirty-five miles west of Aberdeen and three miles south of Mossat on the A97. The castle, now much ruined, occupies a tranquil location on rising ground with pleasant wooded hills rising around. To the rear the lands falls away in a steep ravine known as the Back Den (this is now a superb rock garden located in the grounds of the present Kildrummy Castle Hotel.) Although much of the superstructure has gone, enough of the fine ashlar masonry remains to create a vivid impression of the size and might of the strength of Mar. The castle is polygonal in plan, with a pair of massive gatehouse towers and additional towers studding the curtain at the four major angles. The falling ground to the front and east was protected by a deep ditch, some seventy-five feet across and fifteen feet deep. At the front the ditch was traversed by a causeway and this, as 1950s archaeology revealed, had been crossed by a temporary barbican while the great drum towers of the gateway, the last elements to be constructed, were being built.

The original design featured only the curtain wall, with the round flanking towers added later, but all within the span of the thirteenth century. A range of domestic buildings shelter within the walls, including the spacious chapel which was constructed as part of the later thirteenth-century works. The provision of the flanking towers greatly enhanced the defence overall, permitting the garrison to deluge attackers in the lee of the walls with missiles. The masonry base of each is splayed outward, or 'battered', to defeat attempts at mining.

The visual appearance of the surviving remains is suggestive, on a smaller scale, of the Edwardian castles in Wales, and the great natural beauty of the location belies the castle's turbulent past. Stand within the outline of the great hall and try to envisage the scene over that distant Christmas of 1410, when the lay and ecclesiastical magnates gathered at the Earl of Mar's table. Imagine the fine timber-roofed hall, smoke rising from the central hearth, the bare walls hung with bright tapestries, the long trestles groaning with the earl's bounty, the wine doubtless flowing in abundance. Think then of the men around the high table – for many, this would be their final Christmas, their blood to be so liberally spilt on the field of the Reid Harlaw.

Appendix 2
The Ballad of Harlaw

The Gaelic battle song composed by Lachlann Mor MacMhuirich is contemporary with the action, but the anonymous Lowland poem 'Battel of Harylaw' is much later and does not appear to have been in existence before 1548. It is suggested that the author might have been familiar with Hector Boece's *Scottorum Historiae*, first published in 1526.

In the Gaelic version the Islesmen are victorious, but in the poem it is Mar who seizes the initiative and fights the clans to a standstill, after which they withdraw, leaving him master of the field.

The later ballad 'The Battle of Harlaw' was first published in Allan Ramsay's *Ever Green* of 1724. The version printed below is as it appears in Volume III of *English and Scottish Popular Ballads* (ed. F.J. Child).

The Battle of Harlaw

As I cam in by Dunidier,
An doun by Netherha,
There was fifty thousand Hielanmen
A-marching to Harlaw.

As I cam on, an farther on,
An doun and by Balquhain,
On there I met Sir James the Rose,
Wi him Sir John the Gryme.

'O cam ye frae the Hielands man,
An me cam a' ta wey?
Saw ye Macdonnel an his men,
As they cam frae the Skee.'

'Yes, me cam frae ta Hielands man,
An me cam a' ta way,
An she saw Macdonnel an his men,
As they cam frae to Skee.'

'Oh was ye near to Macdonnel's men?
Did ye their numbers see?
Come, tell to me, John Hielanman
What micht their numbers be?'

'Yes, me was near, and near eneuch,
An me their numbers saw;
There was fifty thousan Hielanmen
A-marching to Harlaw.'

'Gin that be true,' says James the Rose,
'We'll no come meikle speed;
We'll cry upon our merry men,
And lichtly mount our steed.'

'Oh no, oh no,' says John the Gryme,
'That thing maun never be;
The gallant Grymes were never bate,
We'll try phat we can dee.'

As I cam on, an farther on,
An doun an by Harlaw,
They fell fu close on ilka side;
Sic fun ye never saw.

They fell fu close on ilka side,
Sic fun ye never saw;
For Hielan swords gled clash for clash,
At the battle o' Harlaw.

The Hielanmen, wi' their lang swords,
They laid on us fu sair,
An they drave back our merry men
Three acres breadth an mair.

Brave Forbes to his brither did say,
Noo brither, dinna ye see?
They beat us back on ilka side,
An we'se be forced to flee.

'Oh no, oh no my brither dear,
That thing maun never be,
Tak your good sword in your hand,
And come your wa's wi me.'

'Oh no, oh no, my brither dear,
The clans they are ower strang,
An they drive back our merry men,
Wi swords baith sharp an lang.'

Brave Forbes drew his men aside,
Sa'd Tak your rest awhile,
Until I to Drumminnor send,
To fess my coat o' mail.

The servan did he ride,
An his horse it did na fail,
For in twa hours an a quarter
He brocht the coat o' mail.

Then back to back the brithers twa
Gaed in amang the throng,
An they hewed doun the Hielanmen,
Wi swords baith sharp an lang.

Macdonnel, he was young an stout,
Had on his coat o' mail,
An he has gane oot throw them a',
To try his han himself.

The first ae straik that Forbes strack,
He garrt Macdonnel reel,
An the neist ae straik that Forbes strack
The great Macdonnel fell.

An siccan a lierachie
I'm sure ye never saw
As wis amo the Hielanmen,
When they saw Macdonnel fa.

An whan they saw that he was deid,
They turnd an ran awa,
An they buried him in Leggett's Den
A large mile frae Harlaw.

They rade, they ran, an some did gang,
They were o' sma record;
But Forbes an his merry men,
They slew them a' the road.

On Monanday, at mornin,
The battle it began,
On Saturday, at gloamin,
Ye'd scarce kent wha had wan.

An sic a weary buryin
I'm sure ye never saw
As wis the Sunday after that,
On the muirs aneath Harlaw.

Gin any body speer at you
For them ye took awa,
Ye may tell their wives and bairnies
They're sleepin at Harlaw.

Notes

I: BEING INTRODUCTORY

1   These distinctive swords will be discussed in chapter 5 but it should be noted that they are not to be confused with the long-bladed hand and a half sword of the next century, the 'great sword' or *cleadamh mor* ('claymore').

2   The ballad 'The Battell of Harylaw' may be contemporary but was not printed until 1548.

3   From Walter Bower's *Chronicle in Liber Pluscardensis* ed. Skene, F.J.H. (Edinburgh 1877–1880).

4   From Major's *History of Greater Britain*, 1521 (Scottish History Society 1892), and as quoted in Douglas Simpson, W., *The Earldom of Mar* (Aberdeen 1949) pp. 49-50. The Gaelic version of the battle is recounted in the 'MacDonald Battle Song' reproduced in *Highland Papers* i (Scottish History Society 1914). The Lowland version of events is recounted, largely without critical analysis, in numerous of the nineteenth-century works, particularly *The New Statistical Account* xii, 'Aberdeenshire' (Edinburgh 1845). A number of unsubstantiated assertions concerning the events of the battle appear in Davidson, J., *Inverurie and the Earldom of the Garioch* (Edinburgh 1878). A more useful commentary on the Lowland traditions is to be found in Mackay, W., *Sidelights in Highland History* (Inverness 1925). More recent works which consider the battle and surrounding events include Grant, I.F., *The Lordship of the Isles* (reprinted Edinburgh 1982) – the original account, written in the 1930s, is a magical account of the Lordship as seen through reflections during the course of the author's travels in the Highlands and Islands in the 1930s. Further useful commentary is to be found in Nicholson, Ranald, *Scotland, the Later Middle Ages* (Edinburgh 1974) and there is an excellent account of the fighting in Marren, Peter, *Grampian Battlefields* (Aberdeen 1990). The political background is covered in considerable detail in Boardman, S., *The Early Stewart Kings* (East Lothian 1996).

5   Douglas Simpson *op. cit.* p. 49.

6   The earl was the leading tactician behind the Scots ascendancy in the war with England from 1369; however, prior to the Homildon campaign he had quarrelled with the mercurial Rothesay, who had chosen a Douglas rather than a Dunbar marriage alliance. As Rothesay refused to return an earlier dowry, the earl defected to the English. His steady hand may be discerned at Homildon and, by supreme irony, he also appears to have acted as advisor to Henry IV immediately prior to the battle of Shrewsbury, where Hotspur's rebellion was crushed and he was himself slain.

7   Spices, themselves a rare and quite precious commodity, were, in terms of rental income, a useful hedge against inflation of the currency.

8   Barrow, G.W.S., *Robert Bruce* (London 1965) p. 12.

9   Tabraham, C., *Scottish Castles and Fortifications* (Edinburgh 1996) p. 30.

10   Tabraham *op. cit.* p. 31.

11   *Ibid.* p. 32

12   *Ibid*. pp. 35–36.
13   *Ibid*. p. 38.
14   Barrow *op. cit*. p. 14.
15   *Ibid*. pp. 10–11.

2: THE HOUSE OF STEWART

1   Quoted in Boardman *op. cit*. p. xiii.
2   Bingham, C., *The Stewart Kingdom of Scotland* 1371–1603 (London 1974) p. 20.
3   Quoted in Bingham *op. cit*. p. 23.
4   *Ibid*. p. 25.
5   Lynch, M., *Scotland: A New History* (London 1991) p. 132.
6   John was scarcely a name to conjure with. The opprobrium heaped on John Balliol ('Toom Tabard') made the change to the more acceptable name Robert, with its heroic connotations, a politically sound expedient.
7   Lynch *op. cit*. p. 139.
8   *Ibid*. p. 138.
9   Edinburgh was not adopted as the capital until the fifteenth century.
10   This taint of illegitimacy was a possible factor in the subsequent assassination of James I.
11   Balfour-Melville, E.W.M., *James I, King of Scots* 1406–1437 (London 1936) p. 4.
12   Quoted in Lynch, *op. cit*. p. 139.
13   Balfour-Melville *op. cit*. p. 5.
14   *Ibid*. p. 10.
15   Boardman *op. cit*. p. 72.
16   *Ibid*. p. 183.
17   *Ibid*. p. 75.
18   *Ibid*. p. 82.
19   *Ibid*. p. 83.
20   *Ibid*. pp. 85–86.
21   Quoted in Boardman *op. cit*. p. 175.
22   *Ibid*. p. 176.
23   *Ibid*. p. 181.
24   Balfour-Melville *op. cit*. p. 12.
25   The exchequer accounts detail an expenditure of £14 2s 11d on the building of the combatants' arena for *sexaginta personarum pugnacium in Insula de Perth* ('sixty persons fighting upon the Inch of Perth'); quoted in Bingham *op. cit*. p. 30.
26   Balfour-Melville *op. cit*. p. 13.
27   *Ibid*. p. 15.
28   *Ibid*. p. 21.

3: THE LORDSHIP OF THE ISLES

1   Quoted in Grant *op. cit*. p. 27.
2   Quoted in Grant *op. cit*. p. 147.
3   Quoted in Newark, T., *Celtic Warriors* (London 1986) p. 81.
4   Magnus is described as 'an unpeaceful man, who thirsted after others' possessions and thought little of his own'; quoted in Grant *op. cit*. p. 150. The epithet 'Bareleg' refers to the king's fondness for Hebridean dress, something of an anomaly among his Norwegian contemporaries.
5   Literally 'Summer Viking'.
6   Quoted in Newark *op. cit*. p. 63.
7   Casey, D., in *History Scotland* vol. 3 no. 4.
8   Campbell Paterson, R., *The Lords of the Isles* (Edinburgh 2001) p. 3.

9   Campbell Paterson *op. cit.* p. 4.

10   It is impossible that the fight actually took place on the night of 5–6 January as there was insufficient light – more likely the actual date was a week later, the night of 12 January, when there was a full moon.

11   There are no surviving examples of Highland galleys, but these vessels were based upon Viking longships; representations may be found on grave slabs, seals and drawings. The principal differentiation was that Scottish galleys were fitted with a steering rudder, while the Norse precedent relied on a steering oar. Somerled found that the rudder made the boat significantly more manoeuvrable, an inestimable advantage in naval warfare. The Great Seal of Islay and the Isles (1176) shows a galley fitted with a steering rudder.

12   The present remains are no older than the fourteenth century.

13   Islay is said to have been the location of the semi-mythical battle of Ventry ('the White Strand'). The High King of Ireland, Daire Don, led a great host to levy tribute from the Isles but was resisted by the great hero, Finn McCool, and his warband, the Feine. Long and bloody was the fight, as long as a year and a day, spilling over the long ribbon of pure white sand. The battle, in the best Celtic vein, consisted of a series of heroic combats with heavy losses on both sides. The last Irish survivor sought refuge in flight, his vessel skimming over the blue waves to safety, but Cael, Finn's foster son, swam out in pursuit and, despite his many wounds, pulled the Irishman overboard. Both were drowned; see Grant *op. cit.* pp. 292-293.

14   Campbell Paterson *op. cit.* pp. 8-9.

15   *Ibid.* p. 14.

16   Quoted *ibid.* p. 4.

17   *Ibid.* p. 16.

18   Tanistry – the ancient Celtic rule of succession – was designed to ensure that an experienced adult male took control on the death of the incumbent. The candidate was elected from within a class of eligible individuals called tanists, which could include a brother or cousin. In theory, this was to prevent the evils attendant on a royal minority, but it could produce ample bloodletting in the wake of feuding factions; see Grimble, I., *Clans and Chiefs* (London 1980) p. 43 & pp. 45-46.

19   He founded the Macian sept which was established in Ardnamurchan by the fourteenth century; see Campbell Paterson *op. cit.* p. 18.

20   Quoted in Campbell Paterson *op. cit.* p. 20.

21   *Ibid.* p. 21.

22   Quoted in Traquair, P., *Freedom's Sword* (London 1998) p. 152.

23   The Macdonalds of Glencoe were the smallest sept of the clan, settling in a string of hamlets at the western end of the wild and haunting glen. They were not much liked by their neighbours and are most remembered for having been the victims of the infamous massacre of 1692.

24   Campbell Paterson *op. cit.* p. 25.

25   David II received several injuries caused by arrows during the battle; one caused him to suffer violent headaches for years afterward. He was captured by John de Coupland, a Northumbrian knight on the rise, though in the struggle the king knocked out several of his captor's teeth. The knight was amply compensated by the rewards attendant on the prize, though his meteoric rise was subsequently cut short by his neighbours, who saw fit to murder him.

26   Campbell Paterson *op. cit.* p. 26.

27   According to Hugh Macdonald, John did divorce Amie; he was not the man to allow sentiment to outweigh expediency! See Grant *op. cit.* p. 177.

28   Campbell Paterson *op. cit.* p. 28.

29   John made one cardinal error, in that, with Douglas, he appears to have fought in the battle of Poitiers in 1356. At Poitiers an English army under Edward of Woodstock (Edward III's eldest son, the Black Prince) defeated a much larger French force and took a vast haul of prisoners which, besides the king of France, included both Douglas and Macdonald; Grant *op. cit.* p. 176.

30   Quoted Campbell Paterson *op. cit.* p. 30.

31   Quoted *ibid.* p. 30.

32   *Ibid.* p. 28.

33   Hugh Macdonald, writing in the reign of Charles II, provides a lively if not necessarily entirely reliable narrative.

34   Quoted in Campbell Paterson *op. cit.* p. 30.

35   John was a significant benefactor; he made donations to Iona and roofed over chapels on Orsay (off Islay), Finlaggan and Loch Sween. Donald was equally generous in his lifetime; Grant *op. cit.* pp. 117-118.

36   Blackmail or 'Black Rent' was, as the name implies, a means of extortion whereby farmers were obliged to pay off caterans to avoid the wasting of their crops; the Anglo-Scottish border reivers of the sixteenth century elevated this pernicious practice to a major local industry!

37   Grant *op. cit.* p. 179.

38   Campbell Paterson *op. cit.* p. 32.

39   Quoted in Grant *op. cit.* p. 114.

40   Ireland provided a useful change of address for any individual finding matters on the mainland becoming overly contentious and potentially injurious to health and life expectancy.

41   Grant *op. cit.* p. 179.

4: THE EARLDOM OF MAR

1   Quoted in Douglas Simpson *op. cit.* p. 19.

2   Douglas Simpson *op. cit.* p. 18.

3.   The Placita Rolls for the army of Edward I record that two courts martial were held at Kildrummy in that August and that one man convicted of murder was hanged.

4   The work to the great drum towers of the gateway may be Edwardian and, if so, remains the only surviving examples in Scotland. The style of building is strongly suggestive of the great Welsh castles; the gatehouse forms a self-contained block, a 'gemel tower' with twin projections at the front, and in appearance it is very suggestive of Harlech. The architect, the Savoyard James of St George, was working at Linlithgow in 1299 and may well have progressed to Kildrummy. Certain other Edwardian influences have also survived, including a double lancet window inserted in the north-east tower which exhibits shouldered lintels of the 'Caernarvon' type. See Douglas Simpson *op. cit.* p. 23.

5   Quoted in Douglas Simpson *op. cit.* p. 24.

6   Quoted *ibid.* p. 25.

7   Brown, C., *The Second Scottish War of Independence* (Gloucestershire 2002) p. 95.

8   Quoted in Brown *op. cit.* p. 95.

9   Quoted in Douglas Simpson *op. cit.* p. 35.

10   Quoted *ibid.* p. 35.

11   *Ibid.* p. 39.

12   *Ibid.* p. 38.

13   In 1351 Leith gifted to the city of Aberdeen the two famous church bells, 'Lawrence' and 'Mary', that survived in the belfry of St Nicholas until its destruction in the disastrous fire of 1874.

14   Quoted in Douglas Simpson *op. cit.* p. 44. In November 1390 Robert III granted Malcolm Drummond licence to crenellate (permission to construct a castle) a new fortress at Kindrochit, at the strategic crossing of the Clunie Water where the highway from Atholl and Strathmore leads into western Mar.

15   Quoted in Boardman *op. cit.* p. 260.

16   Boardman *op. cit.* p. 260.

17   Quoted *ibid.* p. 260.

18   Quoted *ibid.* p. 260.

19   The Erskine claim was based on Sir Thomas's marriage to Janet Keith, the widowed Countess Isabella's nearest blood relative; she was the great-granddaughter of Earl Donald, who died in 1297. William Keith, the Earl Marischal, was Janet's half-brother and Albany's father-in-law. By late 1402 both Sir Thomas and his son, Sir Robert, were English captives, having been taken at

Homildon, but Crawford entered into an agreement to lend his powerful voice to their claim.

20   Quoted in Boardman *op. cit.* p. 265.

21   Boardman *op. cit.* p. 263.

22   These lands comprised the estate of Tullicurran in Strathardle, the castle of Glenatnay in Perthshire and the kirkton of Eassie in Angus; see Boardman *op. cit.* p. 263.

23   The charter is incorrectly dated 9 September; this should in fact have been stated as 9 December – the later date is confirmed by the notarial instruments.

24   Douglas Simpson *op. cit.* p. 45.

25   Boardman *op. cit.* p. 266.

26   Douglas Simpson *op. cit.* p. 60.

27   *Ibid.* p. 60.

28   Quoted *ibid.* p. 59.

5: CLASH OF SPEARS

1   Quoted in Bingham, C., *Beyond the Highland Line* (London 1991) p. 80.

2   Hill, J.M., *Celtic Warfare 1595–1763* (Edinburgh 2003) p. 1.

3   Hill *op. cit.* p. 1.

4   Clan Donald was a major provider of these renowned Hebridean mercenaries.

5   Boardman *op. cit.* p. 13.

6   Boardman *op. cit.* p. 83.

7   *Ibid.* p. 84.

8   *Ibid.* p. 84.

9   *Ibid.* p. 84.

10   Quoted *ibid.* p. 84.

11   Quoted *ibid.* p. 132.

12   Quoted in Marren *op. cit.* p. 91.

13   *Ibid.*

14   Quoted in Grant *op. cit.* p. 123.

15   *Ibid.*

16   Quoted *ibid.* pp. 206–207.

17   Caldwell, D.H., *The Scottish Armoury* (Edinburgh 1979) p. 8.

18   Norman, A.V.B. & Pottinger, D., *English Weapons and Warfare 449–1660* (London 1966) pp. 111–112.

19   Douglas Simpson *op. cit.* p. 56.

20   Caldwell *op. cit.* pp. 22–23.

21   Ballock knives were so named because the wooden hilt was finished with two globular extrusions at the lower (blade) end; a rondel was a single-edged thin-bladed weapon with a rounded hilt; the quillon dagger had two short downswept quillons like a miniature sword.

22   Caldwell *op. cit.* p. 19.

23   *Ibid.* p. 16.

24   Quoted in Wise, T., *The Wars of the Roses* (London 1983) p. 27.

25   Caldwell *op. cit.* p. 11.

26   *Ibid.* p. 18.

27   Nusbacher, A., *The Battle of Bannockburn 1314* (Gloucestershire 2000) p. 96.

28   Grant, A., 'Disaster at Neville's Cross – The Scottish Point of View' in *The battle of Neville's Cross 1346*, ed. Prestwich, p. 30.

29   Quoted in Boardman, A., *The Medieval Soldier in the Wars of the Roses* (London 1998) p. 173.

30   The Cathar or Albigensian (after the city of Albi in the Pays du Tarn) heresy was a dualist faith allied to Bogomilism and the Waldensians, which flourished in the Languedoc in the late twelfth century. It was brutally suppressed by a series of crusades in the early years of the following century.

31   This was Simon de Montfort's victory over Peter II of Aragon.

32   Perhaps most famous was the siege of one of the Cathar's last great mountain fortresses, Monsegur, in 1244.

33   Quoted in Prestwich, M., *Armies and Warfare in the Middle Ages*, p. 312.

34   Quoted in Reese, P., *Bannockburn* (Edinburgh 2000) p. 146.

35   *Registrum Abbatis Johannis Whethamstede* ed. Riley, H.T. (1872), vol. 1 p. 388.

36   Quoted in Prestwich *op. cit.* p. 313.

37   *Medieval History* (June 2004) pp. 51-52.

38   It is generally supposed that there were few, if any, women on the medieval battlefield, but an interesting anecdote relates that a prehistoric marker known as the Liggar Stone, which stood near to the hamlet from which the battle takes its name, also marked a grave pit into which were laid the dead bodies of a number of females killed in the fight. It is unlikely that these were Gaelic Amazons but more likely water carriers/camp followers, who were unfortunate enough to be cut down in the mêlée.

39   Quoted in Bartlett, C., *The English Longbowman 1330–1515* (London 1995) p. 51.

6: THE FIERY CROSS

1   Boardman, S. *op. cit.* p. 258.

2   According to *The Scots Peerage*, Euphemia did not actually become a nun till 1415, so in 1411 Donald had no legal interest in the earldom; see Grant *op. cit.* p. 180.

3   The Duke of Rothesay had been Earl of Atholl and the title reverted to the Crown on his death; the grant to Albany was therefore in 'free regality' but only for the remainder of Robert III's life.

4   Quoted in Marren *op. cit.* p. 91.

5   The numbers involved are of course purely conjectural. Donald's original picked force of 6,000 is a very similar number to those commanded by Charles Edward Stewart, 'Bonnie Prince Charlie', who penetrated as far south as Derby in the winter of 1745. Donald commanded a far greater level of allegiance than the Young Pretender. Just prior to the last Jacobite uprising, Duncan Forbes of Culloden, Lord President of the Court of Session and one who knew and understood the clans, estimated the total military capacity of the Highlands (including both Whigs and Jacobites) at 31,930 fighting men. Assuming population levels had not altered dramatically in the intervening centuries, a similar total might obtain for 1411. For the Lord of the Isles therefore to raise 6,000 of these is by no means improbable.

6   The Macleans were originally to be found on the mainland around Morvern. Two brothers, Lachlan and Hector, settled on Mull. Lachlan later married John of the Isles's daughter. As befitting close kin, John established his son-in-law at Duart on Mull; a magnificent castle, possibly the finest in the Highlands, now crowns the promontory, 'a castle that has few rivals in the magnificence of its surroundings'; Grant *op. cit.* p. 75.

7   Bruce's savage taking-up or herschip of Buchan drove the Comyns (Cummings) and their kindred into alliance with the Macintoshes. This confederation of minor clans, which included the Davidsons, Macgillvrays and Shaws, became Clan Chattan, the Clan of the Cats. The feline symbol is said to have represented the memory of the cat-headed king of Ireland, Cairbre. The confederation survived until the '45 and Clan Chattan charged and died on Drummossie Moor. See Grimble *op. cit.* p. 65.

8   Prebble, J., *Culloden* (London 1964) p. 41.

9   Grant *op. cit.* pp. 180-181.

10   Balfour-Melville, E.W.M., *James I* (London 1936) p. 38.

11   It is hard to judge if the priest's mission was a success, for he appears never to have returned to the Isles, being taken into James I's household.

12   Quoted in Balfour-Melville *op. cit.* p. 38.

13   A son and daughter of Dartasso's married a daughter and son of the Lord of the Isles; Balfour-Melville *op. cit.* p. 38.

14   Quoted in Grant *op. cit.* p. 181.

15   The university was not founded until 1495, by William Elphinstone. The city's burgh records date back to 1398, the oldest in Scotland. In the fourteenth century the principal church was the twelfth-century St Nicholas and this featured the Drum Aisle, the ancient vault of Irvine of Drum.

The site has now been much rebuilt and comprises an east and a west church; the former was built in 1775 and the latter in 1834, but was substantially renewed after a calamitous fire in 1874.

7: THE REID HARLAW

1   Quoted in Marren *op. cit.* p.93. We have no real idea of numbers for Mar's host, though the chroniclers generally agree he was substantively outnumbered. The ballad credits Donald with 'fifty thousand Hielanmen', a ludicrously high number – the whole of the Highlands could not have produced such a muster. If we accept 6,000 in the original muster, with reinforcements from Ross, then allowing for casualties and deserters (the latter always being high in Highland armies) it might be reasonable to allow Donald 5,000-6,000 men on the field, rather less if we subtract those foraging or otherwise absent. Bower gives Donald 10,000, a suspiciously tidy number; Major suggests odds of ten to one, again far too high – no commander would accept the hazard of battle in such circumstances. As a sensible guess, we could suggest Mar commanded somewhere in the region of 3,000-4,000.

2   Douglas Simpson *op. cit.* p. 51 (n).

3   Quoted in Douglas Simpson *op. cit.* p. 55.

4   *Ibid.* p. 55.

5   *Ibid.*

6   These 'lang swords' are the 'halflang' swords referred to in chapter 5. The famous double-handed sword, the 'great sword' of the Highlanders, was a sixteenth-century development.

7   Quoted in Douglas Simpson *op. cit.* p. 52.

8   Hugh Macdonald goes on to assert that the only further participation from those who sought refuge in the cattle fold was to creep out after dark and rob the dead. This may well be a highly biased view, but scavengers were common on medieval battlefields. It is possible that the cattle fold actually served as a rallying point and the panicked men did not desert the field completely.

9   Quoted in Grant *op. cit.* pp. 182-183.

10 Douglas Simpson *op. cit.* p. 52.

11 Grant (*op. cit.*) feels that this cannot be correct as Donald would be unlikely to place two of his chief allies in the reserves, which is specifically said to have comprised light and nimble men, in effect light infantry. Both Mackenzie and Cameron would expect a place of honour in the line and it was traditional for the best-armed and bravest to stand to the fore. This conclusion appears entirely logical unless Donald had cause to mistrust both; there was, in particular, no love lost with the Mackenzies.

12 Grant *op. cit.* pp. 182-183.

13 The chronicle accounts of the battle of Neville's Cross, for instance, specifically mention several lulls in the combat when both sides, as though by tacit agreement, drew apart to draw breath and attend to their order; see Grant, A. *op. cit.* p. 31.

14 Quoted in Douglas Simpson *op. cit.* p. 52.

15 Quoted in Campbell Paterson *op. cit.* p. 37.

16 Quoted in Marren *op. cit.* p. 93. Davidson, presumably born a commoner, is recorded as Sir Robert; his presence on the field is recorded by Boece, though not Bower, who expressly excludes any reference to him in his list of those gentlemen '*valentes armigeri*' who died in the fight. Dr Douglas Simpson suggests that Mar may have knighted his old friend on the eve of the battle. This is by no means unlikely; see Douglas Simpson *op. cit.* pp. 50-51.

17 Douglas Simpson *op. cit.* p. 182.

18 Keegan, J., *The Face of Battle* (London 1976) p. 103.

19 The Laird of Skene, who had married another daughter of the Earl Marischal.

20 A landholder in the parish of Rayne, whose son and successor Andrew was given full remission on the feudal dues which would otherwise have been levied on his father's estate. Sir Andrew Leslie of Balquhain is said to have left six, or perhaps as many as eleven, of his sons on the field. His castle stood by the road to Chapel o' Garioch and a later sixteenth-century tower now occupies the ground.

21   Quoted in Douglas Simpson *op. cit.* p. 55. The following tribute to Davidson and the other Aberdonians who fell was written in the roll of benefactors of the Town's Kirk of Aberdeen, where the provost had been patron of the chantry chapel of St Ann: 'He was a man brave and bold who prospered in all things, and died in the battle of Harlaw, and with him many praiseworthy burgesses, staunch and steadfast rooted in honest principles and inured in all probity (whose names, for lack of time, and because of errors as to names, cannot now be set down as it were fitting), in defence of the town, and for the liberty of their fatherland, under the banner of Alexander Stewart, Earl of Mar. And the said Robert was buried before the altar of St Ann, in the foresaid parish church. On whose soul may God have mercy'. Quoted in Douglas Simpson *op. cit.* p. 56.

22   Major is probably the most accurate of the earlier writers, even if by no means contemporary: 'The civilised Scots slew Donald's army commander, Maclean, and other nine hundred of his men, and yet more were sorely wounded. Of the southerners, six hundred lost their lives... but in so much as very few escaped without a wound, and the fight lasted long, it is reckoned as hot and fierce'. Quoted in Marren *op. cit.* p. 96.

23   Both Boece and Major avoid any claim that the battle was a Lowland victory; both state that the armies, having drawn apart, each withdrew to the relative security of neighbouring hills and thus neither could claim the field. Dr Douglas Simpson feels that if this was the case then Mar might have fallen back across the Urie to the higher ground of Knockinglews and Dilly Hill, west of Inverurie. This must remain doubtful. It would have been a difficult business for the earl to gather his exhausted and bloodied brigades and draw them off in good order. It does seem more likely that the fighting continued until dusk, the fury of the Highlanders' attacks abating with the onset of darkness and their own exhaustion. To attempt what would be a retreat in the face of an unbroken enemy would have been a highly risky manoeuvre, unwarranted in the circumstances.

24   Quoted in Douglas Simpson *op. cit.* p. 54.

25   Quoted in Paterson *op. cit.* p. 37.

26   Quoted *ibid.* p. 37.

27   The Gaelic *brosnachadh* or incitement to arms for the battle was composed by Lachlann Macruirich, the founder of a line of Clanranald bards (see Campbell Paterson *op. cit.* p. 35). The chant was composed to fire the martial spirit of the Islesmen, to remind them of Clan Donald's long and honourable line, descended as they were from the Irish paladin, Conn of the Hundred Battles. The poem would be recited as a hypnotic chant which progressed through the alphabet in alliterative couplets; the proper sense is completely lost in translation. The singing would have had the accompaniment of the clarsach, the Highland harp (the skirl of the pipes so closely associated with Highland warriors belongs to succeeding centuries). See Bingham, C., *Beyond the Highland Line*, p. 81.

28   Quoted in Campbell Paterson *op. cit.* p. 38.

29   Quoted in Marren *op. cit.* p. 99.

30   Quoted in Douglas Simpson *op. cit.* pp. 49-50.

8: THE RECKONING

1   Quoted in Campbell Paterson *op. cit.* pp. 55-56.

2   Quoted in Campbell Paterson *op. cit.* p. 39.

3   *Ibid.* p. 39.

4   *Ibid.*

5   The murder, which James I later sought to deny, appears to have more to do with a plan to unseat Alexander of the Isles.

6   Quoted in Grant, I.F. *op. cit.* pp. 186-187.

7   Quoted in Grant, I.F. *op. cit.* p. 187.

8   This was Bower's estimate of the number of chiefs involved.

9   Quoted in Bingham, C., *The Stewart Kingdom of Scotland* 1371–1603, p. 53.

10   Grant, I.F. *op. cit.* p. 187.

11   Quoted in Bingham, C., *The Stewart Kingdom of Scotland* 1371–1603, p. 53.

12   Quoted in Grant, I.F. *op. cit.* p. 187.

13   'Alexander was given lovely advice at the council table'; quoted in Bingham, C., *The Stewart Kingdom of Scotland* 1371–1603, p. 53.

14   Grimble *op. cit.* p. 85.

15   On Palm Sunday in Lochaber, the two defecting clans quarrelled and the Clan Chattan men surprised the church in which the Camerons were hearing mass and set it on fire, destroying the building and the entire congregation within! See Grant, I.F. *op. cit.* p. 188.

16   Inverlochy Castle still stands just north of the town centre of Fort William, though it is surrounded by modern light industrial buildings. It was to feature again in another dramatic battle of 1645 when Montrose defeated Argyll and his Campbells in a savage, if brief, fight by the lochside.

17   Quoted in Grant, I.F. *op. cit.* p. 189.

18   For a fuller account from Hugh Macdonald of the battle at Inverlochy see Grant, I.F. *op. cit.* pp. 189-190.

19   Campbell Paterson *op. cit.* p. 44.

20   Quoted in Balfour-Melville, E.W.M., *James I*, p. 184.

21   *Ibid.*

22   The form of indenture entered into between lord and retainer, known as a bond of manrent, is usually seen as a measure of stability in a medieval society; significantly, the first such contract to survive in Scotland was made between the Lord of the Isles and one of his affinity. See Lynch *op. cit.* p. 163.

23   So-called because of a distinctive birthmark which covers half his face, as shown on the contemporary drawing by Jorg von Ehingen.

24   Quoted in Campbell Paterson *op. cit.* p. 46.

25   Despite the assertion as to his mild disposition, Elizabeth was to accuse her husband of her attempted murder while pregnant.

26   Douglas had previously accepted a safe conduct.

27   This forms part of legislation which was intended to strengthen the powers of the Crown in dispensing justice; the powers of the border wardens were limited and various castles were brought directly under royal authority, including Stirling and Dumbarton. See Bingham *op. cit.* p. 84.

28   Quoted in Grant, I.F. *op. cit.* p. 194.

29   Quoted *ibid.* p. 194.

30   Quoted *ibid.* p. 196.

31   Surprisingly, given his record of traitorous dealings, Douglas's life was spared and he was kept in relatively comfortable incarceration for the rest of his days.

32   Campbell Paterson *op. cit.* p. 50.

33   In this the Scots were perhaps anticipating a similar policy to be followed later by the Tudors in their dealings with the Gaelic chieftains of Ireland – a policy of confiscation and regrant on purely feudal tenure.

34   Grant, I.F. *op. cit.* p. 199.

35   Quoted in Grant, I.F. *op. cit.* pp. 223-224. Macleod was offended by the treatment meted out on the occasion of the Feast of Aros on Mull. Here, according to Hugh Macdonald, John Macdonald, the tutor of Moidart, was responsible for the delicate matter of seating the guests according to rank. Having seated all of the Clan Donald representatives present, including bards and physicians, he very uncivilly remarked to the waiting Macleans, Macleods and Macneils that he himself was now about to sit and they, being upstarts and parvenus, could shift for themselves! If other than apocryphal, such an insult would indeed prick the honour of proud Highland chieftains. See Campbell Paterson *op. cit.* p. 51.

36   Grant, I.F. *op. cit.* pp. 200-201.

37   *Ibid.* pp. 202-203.

38   Campbell Paterson *op. cit.* p. 54.

39   Gillespie, stung by the taunt, deliberately sought out Kenneth Mackenzie and engaged in single combat, despite the latter being much the the stronger. He was killed in the fight.

40   Some of the panicked Macdonalds apparently asked a local woman working in the fields if the

river was deep. She replied that it was quite fordable at a certain point, to which she obligingly directed them. The desperate Islesmen plunged in; needless to say, this was the deepest point and most drowned. Those who tried to pull themselves out by clinging to bushes were killed by the avenging sickles of the locals.

41   Lynch *op. cit.* p. 167.

42   Quoted *ibid.* p. 168.

APPENDIX I: THE BATTLEFIELD TODAY

1   Quoted in Marren *op. cit.* p. 99.

2   'At present built up into the wall of the graveyard that surrounds the scanty ruins of the Greyfriars Church at Inverness there is the battered effigy of a knight clad in the armour of the early fifteenth century. The figure is on a heroic scale, and the monument to which it belonged must have been one of exceptional distinction. It can hardly be doubted that in this effigy we have all that now remains from the tomb of the victor of Harlaw. He is represented lying on his back, and though both arms are broken off it can still be seen that the hands were clasped in prayer upon his breast. The head, from which the face has unhappily been smashed away, rests upon a pair of tasselled cushions, the upper one placed diagonally over the lower. The knight wears a pointed bascinet over a large, full camail of chainwork, and a cuirass with a tightly indrawn waist. Over the cuirass is the jupon, or short, close fitting surcoat of the time; this has a straight cut lower edge. His legs are encased in complete plate, with prominent and well formed "genouilleres" or knee-caps. The wide sword belt, or knightly girdle, enriched with embossed square mountings, passes low round the haunches; and there is also a narrow diagonal belt, suspended from the right hip, so as to help in taking the weight of the great sword, whose hilt and quillons are gone. On the other side is the misericord dagger, slung by a small belt or strap, hanging loosely from the girdle. Both feet are broken off, but the spur fastenings remain. The total length of the effigy, which is in yellow freestone, is about seven feet'. Quoted in Douglas Simpson, *op. cit.* pp. 58–59 (n).

3   Quoted in Douglas Simpson *op. cit.* pp. 58–59.

4   Quoted in *ibid.* p. 57.

5   Quoted from the guide to the castle (HMSO 1986) p. 2.

Select Bibliography

Arms & Armour Society Journal, vol. XV no. 1, 'The Fourteenth Century Scottish Sword', by T. Willis

Ashdown, C.H., *British & Foreign Arms and Armour* (1909)

Bain, J. (ed.) *Calendar of Documents relating to Scotland 1108–1509* (1881–1884)

Balfour-Melville, E.W.M., *James I, King of Scots 1406–1437* (1936)

Barbour, John, *The Bruce*, ed. Douglas (1994)

Barrow, G.W.S., *Robert Bruce* (1965)

— *The Kingdom of the Scots* (1973)

Bartlett, C., *The English Longbowman 1330–1515* (1995)

'Battel of Harylaw' (1548)

Bingham, C., *The Stewart Kingdom of Scotland* (1974)

— *Beyond the Highland Line* (1991)

Black, C. Stewart, *Scottish Battles* (1936)

Blair, C., *European Armour* (1958)

Boardman, A., *The Medieval Soldier in the Wars of the Roses* (1998)

Boardman, S., *The Early Stewart Kings* (1996)

Boece, Hector, *The Chronicles of Scotland*, ed. Batho & Husbands (1941)

Bower, *Scotichronicon*, vols 6, 7 & 8, ed. D.E.R. Watt (1991–1999)

Brander, M., *The Making of the Highlands* (1980)

Brown, C., *The Second Scottish War of Independence* (2002)

Brown, M., *James I* (1994)

Browne, J., *History of the Highland Clans*, 4 vols (1838)

Caldwell, D.A., *The Scottish Armoury* (1979)

— (ed.) 'Scottish Weapons and Fortifications 1100–1800' in *Three Medieval Swords from Scotland* by Scott J.G. (Edinburgh 1981)

Campbell Paterson, R., *The Lords of the Isles* (2001)

— *For the Lion, A History of the Scottish Wars of Independence, 1296–1357* (1996)

Chadwick, H.M., *Early Scotland* (1949)

Christison, General P., *Bannockburn* (1960)

Collier, G.F., *Highland Dress* (1948)

Davidson, J., *Inverurie and the Earldom of the Garioch* (1878)

Douglas Simpson, W., *The Earldom of Mar* (1949)

— *Scottish Castles* (1959)

Duncan, A.A.M., *Scotland, the Making of the Kingdom* (1975)

Fisher, A., *William Wallace* (1986)

Fordun, John, *Chronicle of Scotland*, trans. Skene (1872)

Froissart, *Chronicles*, ed. Berners (1924)

Grant, I.F., *The Lordship of the Isles* (1982)

Gregory, D., *History of the Western Highlands and Islands of Scotland* (1975)

Grimble, I., *Clans & Chiefs* (1980)

Hill, J.M., *Celtic Warfare 1595–1763* (2003)

Keegan, J., *The Face of Battle* (1976)

Kermack, W.R., *The Scottish Highlands, A Short History* (1957)

Lang, A., *History of Scotland*, 4 vols (1909)

Linklater, E., *Robert the Bruce* (1934)

Lynch, M., *Scotland: A New History* (1991)

'Macdonald Battle Song' in *Highland Papers* I (Scottish History Society 1914)

Macdonald, Hugh, 'History of the Macdonalds' in *Highland Papers* I (1914)

Macdonald, D.J., *Clan Donald* (1978)

Mackay, W., *Sidelights in Highland History* (1925)

Mackie, J.D., *A History of Scotland* (1964)

Maclean, N., *Warriors and Priests, the History of Clan Maclean 1300–1570* (1995)

Major, John, *A History of Greater Britain* (1892)

Marren, P., *Grampian Battlefields* (1990)

Moncrieffe, Sir I., *The Highland Clans* (1967)

New Statistical Account xii 'Aberdeenshire' (1845)

Newark, T., *Celtic Warriors* (1988)

Nicholson, R., *Scotland, the Later Middle Ages* (1974)

Norman, A.V.B. & Pottinger, D., *English Weapons & Warfare 449–1660* (1966)

Nusbacher, A., *Bannockburn 1314* (2000)

Oakeshott, R.E., *The Archaeology of Weapons* (1960)

— *A Knight and His Weapons* (1964)

Oman, Sir C., *A History of the Art of War in the Middle Ages*, 2 vols (1924)

Prebble, J., *Culloden* (1964)

Prestwich, M., *Armies and Warfare in the Middle Ages* (1996)

— *The Three Edwards* (2001 edn)

Registrum Abbatis Johannis Whethamstede, ed. Riley, H.T. (1872)

Rollason, D. & Prestwich, M., *The Battle of Neville's Cross 1346* (1998)

Rothero, C., *The Scottish & Welsh Wars 1250–1400* (1989)

Sadler, D.J., *Scottish Battles* (1996)

Scottish Art Review, 'Ancient Scottish Weapons', vol. 10 no. 2 (1965)

Seymour, W., *Battles in Britain*, 2 vols (1975)

Smout, T.C., *History of the Scottish People* (1970)

Stewart, Colonel D., *Sketches of the Highlanders of Scotland*, 2 vols (1977)

Tabraham, C., *Scottish Castles and Fortifications* (1986)

'The Book of Clanranald' in *Reliquae Celticae*, vol. 2, ed. MacBain & Kennedy (1894)

Traquair, P., *Freedom's Sword* (1998)

Treece H. and Oakeshott, E., *Fighting Men* (1963)

Vasey, N., *Arms and Armour* (1964)

Wesencraft, C., *The Battle of Otterburn* (1988)

Williams, R., *The Lords of the Isles. The Clan Donald and the Early Kingdom of the Scots* (1984)

Wilkinson, F., *Arms and Armour* (1965)

Wise, T., *Medieval Heraldry* (1980)

— *The Wars of the Roses* (1983)

Wyntoun, Andrew of, *The Original Chronicle*, ed. Amours (1903)

Young P. & Adair, J., *Hastings to Culloden* (1964)

List of Illustrations and Maps

Index

TEMPUS REVEALING HISTORY

Scotland From Prehistory to the Present
FIONA WATSON
The Scotsman Bestseller
£9.99
0 7524 2591 9

Flodden
NIALL BARR
'Tells the story brilliantly' **The Sunday Post**
£9.99
0 7524 2593 5

1314 Bannockburn
ARYEH NUSBACHER
'Written with good-humoured verve as
befits a rattling "yarn of sex, violence and
terror"'
History Scotland
£9.99
0 7524 2982 5

Scotland's Black Death
The Foul Death of the English
KAREN JILLINGS
'So incongruously enjoyable a read, and so
attractively presented by the publishers'
The Scotsman
£14.99
0 7524 2314 2

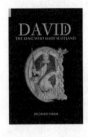

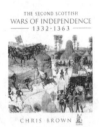

David I The King Who Made Scotland
RICHARD ORAM
'Enthralling... sets just the right tone as the
launch-volume of an important new series
of royal biographies' **Magnus Magnusson**
£17.99
0 7524 2825 X

The Second Scottish War of Independence 1332–1363
CHRIS BROWN
'Explodes the myth of the invincible Bruces...
lucid and highly readable' **History Scotland**
£16.99
0 7524 2312 6

The Kings & Queens of Scotland
RICHARD ORAM
'A serious, readable work that sweeps across
a vast historical landscape' **The Daily Mail**
£20
0 7524 2971 X

Robert the Bruce: A Life Chronicled
CHRIS BROWN
'A masterpiece of research'
The Scots Magazine
£30
0 7524 2575 7